Thatcher Thayer

Some Inquiries Concerning Human Sacrifices Among the Romans.

Thatcher Thayer

Some Inquiries Concerning Human Sacrifices Among the Romans.

ISBN/EAN: 9783743388550

Manufactured in Europe, USA, Canada, Australia, Japa

Cover: Foto ©ninafisch / pixelio.de

Manufactured and distributed by brebook publishing software (www.brebook.com)

Thatcher Thayer

Some Inquiries Concerning Human Sacrifices Among the Romans.

SOME INQUIRIES CONCERNING

HUMAN SACRIFICES

AMONG THE ROMANS.

SOME INQUIRIES CONCERNING

HUMAN SACRIFICES AMONG THE ROMANS.

PRECEDED BY A

REPRINT OF THE CORRESPONDENCE

BETWEEN

MR. MACAULAY, SIR ROBERT PEEL, AND LORD MAHON

UPON THE SAME SUBJECT.

PRINTED, NOT PUBLISHED.

SIDNEY S. RIDER,

PROVIDENCE.

1878.

WERE HUMAN SACRIFICES IN USE
AMONG THE ROMANS?

CORRESPONDENCE

ON THIS QUESTION BETWEEN

MR. MACAULAY, SIR ROBERT PEEL,
AND LORD MAHON.

IN DECEMBER, 1847.

[*NOT PUBLISHED.*]

LONDON:
PRINTED BY SPOTTISWOODE & CO.
New Street Square.
1860.

WERE HUMAN SACRIFICES IN USE
AMONG THE ROMANS?

———·———

I AM induced to print a few copies of the following correspondence, partly from the just value
that must ever attach to any views indicated either
by Lord Macaulay or Sir Robert Peel, and partly
from the great interest of the subject itself. It
may be noticed in these letters that Lord Macaulay discussed the question before him in a more
general manner than did Sir Robert Peel. This,
however, was owing solely to the difference of
their positions at the time. In December, 1847,
Sir Robert had ceased to be a minister or even
in great measure a party chief. Lord Macaulay,
on the contrary, was filling an office involving
very numerous details and accompanied by a seat
in the cabinet. Whenever he had sufficient time
to spare from other tasks, no one loved better to
explore any point of classical antiquity. No man
brought to it a higher amount of critical skill.
Deeply versed as he was in the literature and the

language of both Greece and Rome, and possessing powers of memory far indeed beyond those of ordinary men, it was his delight at every interval of leisure to renew and, if possible, to extend the course of his early reading. As one proof among many of this last assertion, I will allow myself the pleasure of transcribing a passage from a subsequent letter to me of Lord Macaulay. It is dated —

"Clifton, *August 23, 1852.*

"I am certainly much better, and I begin to hope that six weeks more of the Downs will completely restore me. I have been reading a great deal of execrably bad Latin — Suetonius, Vulcatius, Spartianus, Trebellius Pollio, Julius Capitolinus, Lampridius, Vopiscus, — and I am going to try to take the taste of all the barbarisms which I have been devouring out of my mouth, with the 'Andria' and the 'Heauton Timoroumenos.' I have read Herodian too. His Greek is not first rate, but is immeasurably superior to the Latin of his contemporaries. After all there is a great deal to be learned from these writers. Hume was quite in the right when he said that Gibbon ought to have made more of the materials for the 'History of the Empire,' from the Antonines to Diocletian. Indeed, Gibbon very candidly admitted the justice of Hume's criticism".

As to the merits of the controversy on Human Sacrifices at Rome, I must confess myself to remain in a state of considerable doubt. The two passages from Livy and Suetonius, which Sir Robert Peel transmitted to me on the 26th of December, 1847, were not at all within my recollection when I wrote to him on the same day, and they seem but little in accordance with the theory which I then proposed. In the face of such a passage as that from Suetonius, it is not easy to contend that the occasional practice of human sacrifices was entirely unknown, even to the contemporaries and the friends of Cicero. Those who may desire any further to investigate this curious question, will do well to consult a note[1] in the learned and able " History of Christianity," by Dr. Milman.   STANHOPE.

March, 1860.

WERE HUMAN SACRIFICES IN USE AMONG THE ROMANS?

" MONDAY, *December 13, 1847.* — Breakfast at Mr. Hallam's, where I met, amongst others, Mr. and Mrs. Bancroft, Mr. Macaulay, Dr. Milman, and Sir Robert Peel. The party did not break up till nearly one.

" In one part of our conversation, I mentioned a note in a German work which I had lately been reading, the ' History of the Church ' by Dr. Gieseler, Professor of Theology at Göttingen. The note, I said, alleges in substance that human sacrifices existed in the classic days of ancient Rome, and that, as Lactantius states, a man was

[1] Vol. i., page 27.

still in his time immolated every year at the festival of Jupiter Latialis.

"Mr. Macaulay had not seen Dr. Gieseler's book, but declared himself convinced that there was no real foundation for this story. A day or two afterwards, I sent him in a note the exact words of Lactantius as given by Dr. Gieseler: 'Latialis Jupiter etiam nunc sanguine colitur humano.'

"The following correspondence ensued : —

RIGHT HON. T. B. MACAULAY TO LORD MAHON.

"ALBANY, *December 15, 1847.*

"Dear Lord Mahon, — I know nothing of Gieseler, but the passage which you have sent me, and, if I were to form my judgment of him from that passage, I must pronounce him a dunce, or something worse. . . . . In the first place, he misquotes Lactantius. He makes Lactantius say positively, 'Jupiter Latialis is even now propitiated with human blood.' But Lactantius's words are these : 'Ne Latini quidem hujus immanitatis expertes fuerunt, *siquidem* Jupiter Latialis etiam nunc sanguine colitur humano.' I should translate the sentence thus : 'Nor have even the Latins been free from this enormity, if it be true that even now Jupiter Latialis is propitiated with human blood.' It is quite plain to me that Lactantius wished to insinuate what he dared not assert.

"Suppose that there were discovered in the British Museum a Puritan pamphlet of 1641, containing the following passage : 'Nor is even Lambeth free from the worst corruptions of Antichrist, if it be true that the Archbishop of Canterbury and his chaplains pray to an image of the Virgin ;' and suppose that I were to quote the passage thus : 'The Archbishop of Canterbury and his chaplains pray to an image of the Virgin,' — what would you think of my sense or honesty?

" But this is not all. Where did Gieseler find that these human sacrifices were annual, rather than triennial, quinquennial, or decennial? Where did he find that they were performed at Rome, and not at Tibur or Praeneste? Where did he find that the victim was a man and not a woman? Not in Lactantius, I am sure. Yet he quotes no other authority, and I firmly believe that he has none.

" As to the rest, I should certainly never admit the fact on Lactantius's authority, even if he had asserted it in the most positive manner. He was a rhetorician at Nicomedia, writing a party pamphlet in a time of violent excitement. I should think it as absurd to give credit to an affirmation of his in contradiction to the whole literature and history of antiquity, as to believe Mac-Hale when he tells the Irish that the English Government starved two millions of them last year. But, as I have said, Lactantius affirms nothing. He was evidently afraid to do so. Had he had the courage of Gieseler, he would have come out with a gallant barefaced lie.   Ever yours,   T. B. MACAULAY.

SIR ROBERT PEEL TO LORD MAHON.

" DRAYTON MANOR, *December 22, 1847.*

" MY DEAR LORD MAHON, — I thank you for sending me Mr. Macaulay's letter respecting human sacrifices at Rome. If you are interested in the vindication of Dr. Gieseler (of whom I have never heard), you might perhaps find something to say in his defense, though it is rather presumptuous in me to suggest it, first, against such an authority as Mr. Macaulay ; and secondly, because I have neither the passage of the worthy Doctor, which Mr. Macaulay impugns, nor the work of Lactantius, which the Doctor professes to quote. I am aware of no classical authority for the assertion that human sacrifices were offered in classic times at the festival of Jupiter

Latialis. Writers, however, prior to or contemporary with Lactantius, assert the fact in direct terms. Prudentius says : [1]

> "'Funditur humanus Latiari in munere sanguis
> Consessusque ille spectantûm solvit ad aram
> Plutonis fera vota sui.'

"Minutius, who, I believe, lived before Lactantius and Prudentius, and who was probably the authority on whom each of them relied, says: "Quid ipse Jupiter vester ?— cum Capitolinus, tunc gerit fulmina, et cum Latiaris, cruore perfunditur ; " — and, in a subsequent passage, removing any doubt as to the sort of blood, he says expressly : 'Hodieque ab ipsis (Romanis) Latiaris Jupiter homicidio colitur, et quod Saturni filio dignum est, mali et noxii hominis sanguine saginatur.'

"I have no copy of Lactantius, but in the notes of Victor Giselinus, on the passage quoted from Prudentius, there is a quotation from the passage from Lactantius, and it varies from the quotation in Mr. Macaulay's letter in a point not unimportant. As quoted by Giselinus, the passage runs thus : —

"'Galli Hesum et Teutatem humano cruore placabant. Nec Latini quidem hujus immanitatis expertes fuerunt. Siquidem Latialis Jupiter sanguine colitur humano, quid ab his boni precantur qui sic sacrificant ? '

"If the above is a correct quotation, there is perhaps enough of direct assertion on the part of Lactantius to justify the German Doctor in supposing that he meant to assert that the Romans were guilty of human sacrifices.

"But the quotation probably is not a correct one, at least as to punctuation. The words of the original text are, I take for granted, as quoted by Mr. Macaulay : 'Nec Latini quidem hujus immanitatis expertes fuerunt, siquidem Jupiter Latialis etiam nunc sanguine colitur humano."

"Is it quite clear that 'siquidem' must mean *if indeed?* May it not mean *inasmuch as ?* I will give you two passages in which I apprehend it bears the latter construction : 'Siqui-

---

[1] Lib. i., *Contra Symmachum.*

dem e castris egredi non liceret,' is in a passage in Cæsar,[1] of which I think the context will show that *since* or *inasmuch as* is the meaning, and not *if indeed*.

"Ovid, speaking of the illustrious descent and marriage of Peleus, has these lines : —

> "' Nam conjuge Peleus
> Clarus erat Divâ ; nec ari magis ille superbit
> Nomine, quam soceri, *siquidem* Jovis esse nepoti
> Contigit haud uni, conjux Dea contigit uni.'

"Even, however, should my very disinterested plea for the German Doctor avail anything, I do not mean to imply that I agree to the conclusion at which I suppose he has arrived, namely, that there were human sacrifices throughout the classic times of Rome. I cannot reconcile such a conclusion with the silence of the highest classical authorities.

"Such writers as Prudentius, Minutius, and Lactantius were prejudiced against Pagan usages, and readily gave credit to unfavorable reports of them.

"Surely if it had been the annual usage in Rome, in classic times, to offer human victims to Jupiter, Cicero could never have uttered these words: 'Quidquam Gallis sanctum ac religiosum videri potest? Qui etiam si quando aliquo metu adducti, Deos placandos arbitrantur, humanis hostiis eorum aras funestant ut ne religionem quidem colere possint, nisi eam ipsam scelere violarint. Quis enim ignorat eos usque ad hunc diem retinere illam immanem ac barbaram consuetudinem hominum immolandorum ?'

"Now I will release you, being quite ready to offer up Lactantius, Prudentius, and Dr. Gieseler himself, as sacrifices to Cicero.

"I deserve no credit for my parade of learning. One book suggests reference to another, and commentators supply quotations to those who have patience to read them.

"Believe me, very faithfully yours,

"ROBERT PEEL.

---

[1] *De Bello Gallico.*

"On December 26, 1847, I replied at some length to Sir Robert Peel, sending him a literal translation of Dr. Gieseler's note. (Enclosure A.)

"Of the first authority cited in that note I went on to say : —

"Porphyry was known to me by name as one of the later Pagan philosophers, — the pupil of Longinus and the master of Iamblichus. But I was wholly ignorant of his works and contented to remain so. However, my diligence being, as it should be, quickened by Mr. Macaulay's and yours, I have been to a dusty collection, not my own, to look at the original passage, and ascertain the critical character which Porphyry bears ; and I now beg you to accept the result of my research. (Enclosure B.)

"The testimony he gives seems the strongest of all ; and it comes, you will observe, from one who ever since the time he became an author showed himself a bitter enemy of the Christian faith, so that in him the testimony is an admission instead of an accusation.

"I think you have fully established your position as to the meaning of *siquidem.*

"But I confess that I should not quite concur in the cruel immolations which you without pity propose, 'to offer up Lactantius, Prudentius, and Dr. Gieseler himself as sacrifices to Cicero !' It seems to me that the authority of all these writers may be well reconciled, by assuming that a human victim may have been among the Peregrina Sacra — the *externæ cærimoniæ*, — which we know crept into a large extent after the time of Hadrian. They had begun even under Tiberius, though probably not extending to such enormities, as we learn from Tacitus[1] and Suetonius.[2] In some reigns, as under Heliogabalus, the foreign appear to have even predominated over the old national rites.

---

[1] *Annal.*, lib. ii., c. 85.　　　　[2] *Vita Tib.*, c. 38.

" I must own, however, that on my supposition the shrine of Jupiter Latialis is probably the very last where one might expect to meet with these Peregrina Sacra.

"There is another objection to my own theory which occurs to me, and which (though I retain the theory) I will frankly state : Last winter, when reading through the series of the 'Christian Apologies,'[1] I observed that all of them, from the earliest to the latest, felt it necessary to notice and to rebut the accusation that the Christians in their nightly conclaves used to immolate a child. Absurd as we know this accusation to be, we can easily explain its existence from the heathen misapprehension of the terms in which they heard of the Holy Eucharist. But would this accusation have been so fiercely and repeatedly urged if the Pagans themselves had been conscious of human sacrifices at their yearly festivals ?

"It is curious that the classical controversy now before us should have a direct bearing on the history of America, for it has been often debated, in reference to the accounts of early Mexico, how far the practice of human sacrifices can possibly coexist with any high degree of civilization and refinement.

ENCLOSURE (A) IN LORD MAHON'S LETTER OF DECEMBER 26, 1847.

" *Translation from the German of Dr. Gieseler's note as it stands in the first editions of his 'Kirchen-Geschichte.'*[2]

" According to Porphyry[3] human sacrifices among the divers nations ceased in the time of Hadrian ; but even in Porphyry's own time (about 280 after Christ), a human being was immolated every year in Rome to Jupiter Latialis. Lactantius (about 300 after Christ), in his 'Divin. Inst.,' i. c. 21, has these words : 'Latialis Jupiter etiam nunc sanguine colitur humano.'

---

[1] Tertullian, Minutius Felix, etc.   [2] Vol. i., p. 26.
[3] *De Abstinentiâ Carnis*, ii. c. 36.

ENCLOSURE (B) IN LORD MAHON'S LETTER OF DECEMBER
26, 1847.

"The following passage occurs in Porphyry,[1] ed. de Foge-
rolles, Lugdun, 1620. See in that work, lib. ii., p. 225.

" Καταλυθῆναι δὲ τὰς ἀνθρωποθυσίας σχεδὸν τὰς παρὰ πᾶσι φησὶ
Πάλλας (ὁ ἄριστα τὰ περὶ τῶν τοῦ Μίθρα συναγαγὼν μυστηρίων)
ἐφ' Ἀδριανοῦ τοῦ αὐτοκράτορος. Ἐθύετο γὰρ καὶ ἐν Λαοδικεία τῇ
κατὰ Συρίαν τῇ Ἀθηνᾷ κατ' ἔτος παρθένος, νῦν δὲ ἔλαφος, κ. τ. λ.

Ἀλλ' ἔτι καὶ νῦν τὶς ἀγνοεῖ κατὰ τὴν μεγάλην πόλιν τῇ τοῦ Λατ-
ναρίου Διὸς ἑορτῇ σφαζόμενόν ἄνθρωπον;[2]
" The following (and much besides), respecting the life and
character of Porphyry, is told by Fabricius:[3] —

"'Porphyrius Tyrius fuit, patrio nomine Malchus Syrorum
linguâ appellatus, discipulus Longini primum Athenis eruditis-
simi usque quaque viri. . . . . Natus est anno Christi 233,
obiit Romæ postremis annis Diocletiani Imperatoris. . . . .
Licet quoque fuisset primitus Christianus ut Socrates[4] testatur
et Augustinus[5] innuit, acerbus tamen postea ac vehemens
Sacræ Religionis nostræ evasit hostis et insectator.'

" In a letter to me upon another subject, dated
the same day as mine (December 26, 1847), Sir
Robert Peel adds, upon the question of human
sacrifices : —

"What say you to the following passages in Livy and Suetonius ?

[1] Libri v., *De Abstinentiâ Carnis,* περὶ ἀποχῆς ἐμψυχῶν.

[2] " And Pallas (who has collected the best information regarding
the mysteries of Mithras) says that human sacrifices were abolished
in the time of the Emperor Hadrian. For at Laodicea in Syria, it
was the custom to sacrifice annually a maiden to Athena, but now
a deer (is sacrificed), etc. But even now who is ignorant that in
the great city a man is slain on the festival of Jupiter Latiaris ? "

[3] *Bibliotheca Græca,* vol. iv., p. 181, ed. 1711.

[4] *Hist. Eccles.,* lib. iii., c. 23.

[5] *De Civitate Dei,* lib. x., cap. 28.

" Livy, lib. xxxii., cap. 57 : —

" ' Interim ex fatalibus libris sacrificia aliquot extraordinaria facta ; inter quæ Gallus et Galla, Græcus et Græca, in foro boario sub terrâ vidi demissi sunt in locum saxo conseptum jam ante hastiis humanis, minime Romano Sacro, imbutum.'

" Suetonius, Octavius : —

" ' Scribunt quidam trecentos ex dedit illis electos utriusque ordinis ad aram Divo Julio extructam Idibus Martiis hostiarum more mactatos.'

" I do not know what was the precise assertion of Dr. Gieseler, or to what periods of Roman History he refers.

RIGHT HON. T. B. MACAULAY TO LORD MAHON.

" ALBANY, *December 27, 1841.*

" DEAR LORD MAHON, — I return the extract from Porphyry. It is very strong. But I am not convinced. I have spent half an hour in looking into my books, and I feel quite satisfied that there is no foundation for this Eastern story about the Italian worship. The best account of the origin of the feast of Jupiter Latialis — otherwise called Feriæ Latinæ, — which I have found, is in Dionysius. The object of the institution seems to have been political. The solemnity was common to all the cities of Latium, and was meant to bind them together in close alliance. The rites, says Dionysius, were celebrated in the Alban Mount. Every member of the confederation furnished a contingent towards the expenses. Now observe : —

" ' Ταύτας τὰς ἑορτάς τε καὶ τας Θυσίας μέχρι τῶν καθ᾽ ἡμᾶς χρόνων τελοῦσι Ρωμαῖοι, Λατίνας καλοῦντες· καὶ φέρουσιν εἰς ταύτας αἱ μετέχουσαι τῶν ἱερῶν πόλεις, αἱ μὲν, ἄρνας αἱ δέ, τυροὺς' αἱ δὲ, γάλακτός τι μέτρον · αἱ δὲ ὅμοιόν τι τούτοις πελάνου γένος' ἑνὸς δὲ ταύρου κοινῶς ὑπὸ πάντων δυομένου, μέρος ἑκάστη τὸ τεταγμένον λαμβάνει.'¹

¹ "The Romans observe these festivals and sacrifices up to our own times, calling them Latin ; and the cities which participate in

" Now can anybody believe that Dionysius, who had been at Rome, would have written thus if a human sacrifice had been part of the rite ?

" You mentioned Cicero's strong expressions about the aversion of the Romans to human sacrifices. But observe that Cicero himself had officiated as Consul at the feast of Jupiter Latialis. He described the solemnity incidentally in his poem on his own Consulship. You will find the passage in the first book 'De Divinatione.' He introduces Urania speaking to him : —

> " ' Tu quoque cum tumulos Albano in monte nivales
> Lustrasti, et læto mactasti lacte Latinas.'

" This mention of the milk exactly agrees with Dionysius's account. But can you believe that, on this occasion, Cicero sacrificed a man, and thus described the ceremony as one performed læto lacte ? In short, do you believe that Cicero ever sacrificed a man ? I must stop. I have to preside at the Chelsea Board to-day.

"Ever yours,   T. B. MACAULAY.

SIR ROBERT PEEL TO LORD MAHON.

" DRAYTON MANOR, *January 4, 1848*.

" MY DEAR LORD MAHON, — I return to you the enclosed letter from Mr. Macaulay.

" I doubt whether there is to be found among unprejudiced contemporary writers any evidence on which you could convict the Romans of offering human sacrifices during the classical times of Roman history.

" I think, if the practice had prevailed, there would have been such evidence. The Peregrina Sacra were in later times the religious rites contribute to these, some giving lambs, others cheeses, others a certain quantity of milk, and others a certain kind of sacrificial cake equivalent to these ; and when a bull is slain by all each city receives the part assigned."

solemnized in Rome, but the Romans appear to have been adverse to their solemnization. I can find no evidence that human victims were offered at these Peregrina Sacra; and had they been offered, it is still more probable that conclusive evidence of the fact would have been left on record. I must, at the same time, observe that there are among classical writers many vague allusions to expiatory or propitiatory human sacrifices.

"In the cases of some offenses — punishable by death, — there appears to have been, in the earlier times of Rome, a tendency to offer up the victim of the law as a sacrifice to some God; at least to confound the notions of legal punishment with expiatory sacrifice. Mention is somewhere made of a person convicted of *proditio* — and punishable with death — being offered up as a sacrifice to Pluto. In Livy [1] is the following passage: 'Illud adjiciendum videtur licere Consuli Dictatorique et Prætori cum legiones hostium devoveat non utique se, sed quem velit ex legione Romanâ scriptâ civem devovere,' etc., etc.

"I add a curious passage from Dion Cassius.

"The two men to whom he refers were probably mutinous soldiers and punished capitally for mutiny. I only refer to it for the purpose of establishing my position, that there are passages in classical writers which would warrant the impression that, in early periods of Roman history, human sacrifices, for the purpose of propitiation, were deemed to be efficacious.

"I doubt whether there is any conclusive evidence to the fact of human sacrifices in contemporary classical authorities speaking of their own knowledge.

"Believe me, my dear Lord Mahon,
"Very faithfully yours,
"ROBERT PEEL.

"There is a passage in Florus, I think, in which

---

[1] Lib. viii., cap. 1.

he speaks of *humanæ hostiæ* offered by the Samnites, but it is a mere general charge.

ENCLOSURE IN SIR ROBERT PEEL'S LETTER OF JANUARY 4, 1848.

" Dion Cassius, lib. xliii.[1]

"Ἄλλοι δὲ δύο ἄνδρες ἐν τρόπῳ τινὶ ἱερουργίας ἐσφαγήσαν. Καὶ τὸ μὲν ἄιτιον οὐκ ἔχω εἰπεῖν (οὔτε γὰρ ἡ Σιβυλλα ἔχρησεν, οὔτ' ἄλλο τι τοιοῦτον λόγιον ἐγένετο), ἐν δ' οὖν τῷ 'Αρείῳ πεδίῳ πρός τε τῶν ποντιφίκων και πρὸς τοῦ Ἄρεος ἐτύθησαν, καὶ γε αἱ κεφαλαὶ αὐτῶν πρὸς τὸ βασίλειον ἀνετεθήσαν.[2]

" Mr. Hallam, in a letter to me dated Wilton Crescent, January 18, 1848, mentions his recent visit to Drayton Manor, and goes on to say : —

" The party consisted of Lord Aberdeen and his youngest son, Goulburn, the Bishop of Oxford, Buckland, and Eastlake, with Lord and Lady Villiers. . . . . Sir Robert mentioned the sacrificial correspondence, but without giving any more decisive opinion than he had done. He showed me the passage in Dion Cassius,[8] which certainly mentions a human sacrifice by Cæsar, though with some surprise ; but perhaps his surprise is more on account of no sufficient reason being known for than from its being absolutely unheard of. The Bishop of Oxford observed that Porphyry's expression, τίς ἀλνοεῖ? is often used when men assert what is not true, without giving an instance. And certainly it is not uncommon now to hear 'every body knows' about that of which most people know nothing."

[1] *Jul. Cæsar.*
[2] See p. 152.
[8] Lib. xliii., cap. 24.

SOME INQUIRIES CONCERNING HUMAN SACRIFICES AMONG THE ROMANS.

HUMAN SACRIFICES AMONG THE ROMANS.

————•————

AMID all we had to show in our Centennial, we doubt if a group of American Senators could have been found capable of discussing such questions in Classical Antiquity as members of the British Parliament seem to treat with graceful ease and assured acquisition. A pamphlet printed but not published contains letters from Lord Macaulay, Sir Robert Peel, and Lord Mahon, on the subject of Human Sacrifices among the Romans. Macaulay denies their existence, at least in public, so late as the time of Cicero. Gieseler in his " Ecclesiastical History," had quoted Lactantius as affirming that human sacrifices were offered to Jupiter Latialis. Macaulay, as is often his wont, indulges in captious criticism upon the German, and is querulously severe against the Latin Father. He questions Gieseler's interpretation of the particle " siquidem " used by Lactantius, and maintains that it has only a conjectural sense, but he is not

careful to remember that this word, like the corre-
sponding Greek one, is often used to introduce a
strong assertion. Besides, he has not noticed that
Lactantius elsewhere (as we shall see) makes the
same statement without the use of "siquidem."
In reply to a letter of Lord Mahon supporting
Gieseler's view by a passage from Porphyry, he
admits its strength, but clings to his opinion, as
is usual with this popular writer on such occasions.
The matter itself is interesting in various aspects,
and may well invite inquiry. Rome embodies so
much of human history, illustrates so thoroughly
human nature, and has influenced so extensively
human destiny, that we naturally seek to know all
the usages of the greatest national life in the ancient world; and yet we approach this investiga-
tion under some disadvantages. Perhaps, from
reaction, we are in one of those periods occasion-
ally recurring, in which there is quite a disposition to exalt Paganism and lose sight of its
most revolting features. Then, too, the contem-
plation of power hinders moral discrimination in
others than Englishmen and German exalters of
"might." We all feel that wondrous spell of
Rome which confused the conscience of Gibbon,
and sometimes made his sentences a splendid tis-
sue of sophisms. But there is material enough
to form a fair judgment, and Macaulay too might
have found Germans whose researches he could
not have dismissed so summarily as he did those

of Gieseler. Thus Döllinger,[1] after dwelling on "the innumerable indications preserved both in rites and in the sagas bearing abundant testimony to the fact of human sacrifices having been offered by the Romans and races kindred to them in prehistoric times,"[2] adds: " But it was not always that human sacrifice was supplied by these unbloody representatives. In spite of the disinclination manifested by the Romans to such victims, and the dislike with which they observed the use of them among other nations, they themselves had frequent enough recourse to the same means of propitiation." Then he cites Livy, 22, 57, when, in 227 B. C., by decree, "a man and woman of each of two nations (Greek and Gaul) were buried alive in the Forum;" then he adds: " Though Livy speaks of it as a thoroughly unknown sacrifice, yet it was often repeated. Plutarch mentions a similar one.[3]

In the year 95 B. C., indeed, all human sacrifices were interdicted by decree of the Senate. Up to that time, as Pliny says, they had been performed in public ; but on extraordinary occasions it was thought admissible to set aside this prohibition, and the same Pliny observes that instances of it had occurred in his time.[4]

---

[1] *Gentile and Jew in the Courts of the Temple of Christ,* vol. ii., p. 85.

[2] See his reference to Ovid, *F.,* v. 621.

[3] Plutarch, *Marcellus,* 3 ; *Orosius,* 4, 13.

[4] Pliny, *H. N.,* 28, 111.

There was a particular form of prayer for this kind of sacrifice when carried into effect by burying alive, which the master of the college of the Quindecemviri had to repeat first, and the peculiar force of which made itself felt by every one who read it. In times of violence and disturbance the idea of a strange effectiveness in human sacrifice always returned upon the people. Once when. a tumult was raised by Cæsar's soldiers in Rome, two of them were sacrificed to Mars by the pontiffs and the flamen martialis, and their heads were fixed upon the Regia, the same as in the sacrifice of the October horse.[1]

Besides this, the Romans were familiar with the notion of offering human lives as victims of atonement for the dead. This was the object with which Gladiatorial games had begun.[2]

In the slave war Spartacus took a heavy revenge, when he dedicated to his fallen comrade Crexus a mortuary offering of three hundred Roman prisoners, whom he made to fight around the funeral pile.[3] The Triumvir Octavius afterwards competed with the slave general, when he caused three hundred prisoners to be put to death as an offering of expiation at the altar of Divus Julius, on the surrender of Perugia.[4]

---

[1] Dio. Cass., 43 : 24.   [2] Valer. Maximus, 2 : 4-7.
[3] App., *Bell. Civ.*, i. 424 ; Florus, iii. 20 ; Oros., v. 24.
[4] Dio. Cass., 48, 14 ; Suetonius, *Octav.*, 15; Seneca, *De Clem.*, i. 11 ; Zonar, 10 : 21.

The fact has been doubted on the ground that the time and manners of the age would not have suffered it;[1] but the evidence is far too strong. The previously mentioned example of a sacrificial murder, committed by the most distinguished Roman priests in the heart of Rome on Roman soldiers, shows how little custom was a restraint, and the time was that of the proscriptions in which citizen blood was poured out like water. Sextus Pompeius, too, had men thrown alive into the sea along with horses, as an oblation to Neptune, at a time when his enemies' fleet was destroyed by a great storm.[2]

Caligula's having innocent men dressed out as victims and then thrown down precipices, as an atonement for his life, was indeed the act of a blood-thirsty tyrant; but it shows what ideas were abroad.[3]

In the year 270, A. D., further proof was given that, in spite of the late decree issued by Hadrian, recourse was still had from time to time to this means of appeasing the angry gods in dangers threatening the state, when on an irruption of the Marcomanni the Emperor Aurelian offered the Senate to furnish it with prisoners of all nations for certain expiatory sacrifices to be performed.[4]

But there was also a standing sacrifice of the

---

[1] Druman's *Geschichte Rom.*, i., 412.
[2] Dion Cassius, xlviii. 48.
[3] Sueton., *Calig.*, 27.
[4] Vopiscus Aurelius.

kind. The image of Jupiter Latialis was annually sprinkled with human blood. That shed by the gladiators in the public games was used for the purpose. A priest caught the blood in a cup from the body of one who was just wounded and threw it when still warm in the face of the image of the god. This was of regular occurrence, still, in the second and third centuries after Christ. Tatian amongst many others speaks of it as an eye-witness.[1]

To the same effect writes Seppo in his " Heidenthum und dessen bedeutung für das Christenthum."[2] " In Keinem Staate finden wir so vielfältige Erlasse wider die Menschenopfer, wie zu Rom, zum Beweise, dass alle dessfallsigen Verordnungen ausser Wirksamkeit geblieben waren. .... Aus Macrobius 1, 7, geht hervor, dass schon von den ersten Zeiten der Römischen Republik an jährliche Menschenopfer stattgefunden und Porphyrius, Abst. ii. 56, bestätigt diese Übung noch von seiner Zeit. Wer weiss es nicht, ruft Eusebius[3] aus, dass auch jetzt noch in der grossen Stadt dem Jupiter Latiaris ein Mensch geopfert wird. Eben so bezeugen die anderen Väter[4] dass

---

[1] Auct. *Libr. de Spectac. post Cyprian. opp.*, p. 3 ; Minuc. Octav., xxi. 30 ; Tertull., *Adver. Gnost.*, 7 ; *Apol.*, 11 ; *De Spect.*, 6 ; Just. Mart., *Apol.*, 2, 12 ; Lact., i. 21 ; Tatian, c. 46 ; Athan., *Adv. Gr.*, c. 25 ; Fermic., *Mater.*, 26.

[2] Vol. ii., pp. 132–139, §§ 61, 62.

[3] *Præp. Evgl.*, iv. 18.

[4] Tertull., *Apol.*, 9 ; Lact., i. 21–3 ; Minuc. Felix, *Octav.*, p. 34.

noch bis in's vierte Jahrhundert der Christlichen-
Zeit, wie im Saturnischen Alter gewisse Menschenopfer üblich waren, doch so, dass man bei Begehung
der Latiner-ferien in der grossen Stadt verworfene
Menschen unter dem namen 'Bestiarii' Kämpfe
mit wilden Thieren bestehen und sie darin um-
kommen liess. Man nannte diess ebenfalls 'Homi-
cidium' wie Tertullian,[1] und Minucius Felix,[2] ver-
sichern. Wenn gleich die Haruspices gewöhn-
lich nur Opferthiere (Haruga-hostia) gebrauchten
und deren Eingeweide beschauten, so finden wir
doch [3] von einem Tribun erzählt, dass er selbst
ein Kind aus Mutterleib geschnitten, um des Rei-
ches Zukunft zu erforschen. Merkwürdig genug
traf man,[4] in Cäsars Tagen, als auf den Antrag der
Auguren die Heiligthümer der Isis und des Sera-
pis auf dem Marsfelde nieder gerissen werden soll-
ten, und man aus Versehen den Tempel der römischen Schlacht-göttin abbrach, in diesem Schüsseln
mit Menschen-fleisch..... Zwar liessen M. und
J. Brutus 488 u. c. an die Stelle der Menschenopfer
Kämpfe auf Leben und Tod treten, auch erliess
der Senat 657 u. c. 97 v. Chr. geradezu ein Verbot
gegen die Menschenopfer,[5] und Augustus sowohl
als Tiberius,[6] so wie Hadrian,[7] erneurten dasselbe:
aber es fruchtete um so weniger, als selbst die

---

[1] *Apol.*, 9.
[2] xxx. 4.
[3] *Annot. des Amm. Marcell.*, xxix. 9.
[4] Nach Diodors *Zeugniss*, xlii. 26.
[5] Plin., xxx. 3.
[6] Sueton., *Claud.*, 25.
[7] Lactant., *Inst.*, 1.

Kaiser sich nicht daran hielten. Bei Cäsars Tri-
umphfeier 708 u. c. wurden zwei der aufrührischen
Soldaten durch die Hand der Pontifices den Flam-
men des Mars auf dem Marsfelde geopfert und
ihre Köpfer an die Königsburg geheftet.[1] Octavian
selbst liess nach seinem Siege über Antonius und
der Einnahme von Perusia dem Divus Julius auf
einem errichteten Altar nicht weniger als 300 oder[2]
400 auser wählte Ritter und Senatoren von denen
welche sich ihm ergeben mussten, am 15 März 713
u. c. wie opferthiere abschlachten, auf dass sie
zum Sühnopfer für die Seele des Vestorbenen
dienten.[3]   Sextus Pompeius liess dem Neptun
zum Opfer Menschen in's Meer werfen.[4] Zu glei-
chem Zwecke wurden auch Gladiatoren Kämpfe
an den Scheiterhaufen vornehmer Römer veran-
staltet, denn das Blut der Gefallenen sollte den
Manen der Abgeschiedenen zur Erquickung dienen.[5]   Caligula liess einen Gladiator, der sein
Leben zu opfern gelobt hatte, mit einem Kranze
von Opferkraut und einer Binde geschmückt von
den Priester Knaben durch Roms Strassen führen,
worauf er sich vom Collinischen Hügel stürtze,[6]
auch zwang er alle welche während seiner Krank-
heit für ihn zu sterben gelobt hatten, nach seiner

---

[1] δύο ἄνδρες ἐν τροπῳ τινι ἱερουργίας. Dion Cassius, xl. 24 ; xliii. 24.
[2] Nach Dion, xlviii. 45.
[3] Strabo, *Oct.*, 15.   [4] Dion, xlviii., 45.
[5] Tertullian, *De Spect.*, 12 ; Lactant., vi. 20 ; Valer. Max., xi. 4 ;
Cyrillus, *Adv. Jul.*, iv. 128.
[6] Calig., 27.

Genesung wirklich zum Tode. Nero opferte, durch
einen Cometen erschreckt und durch seinen Stern-
deuter Babilus dazu bestimmt, zur Abwendung des
Unheils von seiner Person eine Anzahl vornehmer Römer.[1] Der blühender Antinous bringt,
wie Spartian[2] meldet, sich persönlich für Kaiser
Hadrian zum Opfer dar. Hadrian untersagte zwar
die Menschenopfer im dienste des Mithras aber
Commodus Opferte in denselben Mysterien nach
Lampridius[3] einen Menschen mit eigener Hand.
Gleiches gilt nach Dios Zeugniss,[4] von Didius
Julianus. Heliogabal endlich liess Hunderte von
Kindern vornehmer Familien aus ganz Italien zu-
sammen suchen und nach Rom bringen, um sie
in seinen syrischen Mysterien zuopfern, und ver-
ubte sonach einen heidnischen Kindermord im
Grossen.

Prof. Ernst von Lasaulx, Prof. der Alten Lit-
erat. und D. Z. Rector der Jul. Max. Univers. zu
Würzburg, in his " Beitrag zur Religions Philos-
ophie," treats of " Die Sühnopfer der Griechen
und Römer und ihr Verhältniss zu dem Einen auf
Golgotha." After considering human sacrifices
among the Greeks, he writes on p. 10, " Diesel-
ben religiosen Ideen liegen den Menschenopfern
in alten Rom zu Grunde.[5] Wie in Athen des

---

[1] Suet., *Nero*, 36.   [2] Hadrian, 14.
[3] In *Vita Comm.*   [4] 37, 30 ; 73, 16 ; 79, 71.
[5] Dionysius, i. 38 ; Ovid, *Fast.*, v. 621 ; Macrob., *Sat.*, i. 7, p.
240 ; Lactant. i. 21 ; Minuc. Felix, *Octav.*, 30 ; Arnobius, ii., p. 91.

Erechtheus Töchtern und Kodrus freiwillig sich
zu Sühnopfern darbrachten : so gieng in Rom,
um aus vielen Beispielen eines zu nennen, der
Consul P. Decius im lateinischen Kriege freiwillig
in den Opfertod, indem er sich für seine Legionen
weihte.[1] Statt solcher freiwilliger Opfer wurden
später Gefangene, von den Etruskischen Tarquin-
iern in Jahre d. St. 397 — auf Einmal dreihundert
sieben gefängene Römer mit Punischer Grausam-
keit hingeopfert.[2] So oft irgend eine grosse und
allgemeine Calamität die Existenz des Römischen
Staates bedrohte, wurden auf Befehl der Schick-
salsbücher menschliche Sühnopfer dargebracht,
und ein Gallier und eine Gallierin, ein Grieche
und eine Griechin, oder von welchem anderen
Volke sonst Gefahr drohte unter magischen Ge-
betsformeln, welche der Vorsteher des Collegiums
der Fünfzehnmänner vorsprach [3] auf dem Rinder-
markt lebendig begraben.[4]   Erst im Jahre d. St.
657–97 vor Chr. erliess der Senat ein Decret worin
die Menschenopfer verboten wurden ; [5] dessen un-
geachtet aber lesen wir, dass der Dictator J. Cæsar
im J. 708–46 vor Chr. zwei Menschen mit den her-
kömmlichen Feierlichkeiten durch die Pontifices
und den Flamen Martis auf dem Marsfelde opfern [6]
und dass Augustus nach Besiegung des L. Antonius vierhundert Senatoren und Ritter an den Iden

---

[1] Liv., viii. 9, 10.   [2] Liv., 15.   [3] Plin., xxviii. 3.
[4] Liv., xx. 57 ; Plutarchus, *Marcello*, p. 299; *C. und Mor.*, p. 283.
[5] Plin., xxx. 3.   [6] Dion Cassius, xliii. 24.

des Marz 713–43 vor Chr. auf dem Altar des ver-
götterten Julius hinschlachten liess.[1] Auf gleiche
Weise liess Sextus Pompeius nicht nur Pferde, son-
dern auch Menschen in's Meer werfen dem Nep-
tunus zum Opfer.[2] Ja noch unter Hadrianus starb
der schöne Antinous als freiwilliges Menschenopfer für den Kaiser,[3] und die dem Jupiter Latiaris
auf dem Albanerberg jährlich dargebrachten Menschenopfer sollen bis in's dritte Jahrhundert un-
serer Zeitrechnung fortgedauert haben."[4]

So, too, in a discourse delivered at the anniver-
sary of Guil. Ernest, by Hen. Guil. Vent, the author,
discussing this subject and after quoting Pliny's
claim for the Romans' abolition of these " monstra,"
yet concludes: " Attamen ne illo quidem tempore
omnes superstitionis istius radices evulsæ sunt,
cujus reliquiæ etiam post Augusti tempora anim-
advertuntur. Compressus modo et cohibitus, non
etiam existinctus est inhumanus cultus. Neroni
Imperatori artibus magicis obstricto, homines immolare etiam jucundissimum fuisse idem Plinius
commemorat.[5] Ipsa ultima imperii Romani ætate

---

[1] Dion Cassius, xlviii. 14; Sueton., *Octav.*, 15; Seneca, *De Clem.*, i. 11.

[2] Dion Cassius, xlviii. 48.

[3] Xiphilinus, p. 356, 21 ; Sylb., *Æl. Spartianus Hadriano*, 14; Aurel., *Victor de Cesar*, 14.

[4] Porphyr., *De Abst.*, ii. 56; Justinus Martyr, *Apol.*, ii., p. 100 D ; Theoph., *Ad Autol.*, iii., p. 412 E ; Tatianus, *Adv. Græc.*, p. 284 B ; Euseb., *De Laud. Const.*, 13, 5, p. 1198; Zimmerm., Tertull. *Apol.*, 8, und Scorp. *Adv. Gnos.*, 7 ; Minuc. Felix, *Octav.*, xxi. 15 ; xxx. 4; Lact., i. 21–30 ; Prudent., *Adv. Symmach.*, i. 380.

[5] *H. N.*, xxx. 6.

veterem consuetudinem nonnunquam relatam et
aras hominum sanguine inquinatas legimus."
Professor Tholuck, in his elaborate articles on
heathenism, translated by Professor Emerson in
the " Biblical Repository,"[1] does not except Rome
from the nations practicing " this frightful custom" of human sacrifices, but quotes[2] authors
referred to by others in proof of later human sacrifices.

Creutzer, in volume i., page 258, of his " Sym-
bolik," writes in relation to the Mithriac worship:
" Pallas[3] erzählt uns, Hadrianus habe durch ein
Edict die Menschenopfer fast gänzlich aufgeho-
ben. Dass dieses Verbot auch die Mithriaca
betraf, zeigt der ganze Zusammenhang. Auch
der Orient huldigte dem Mithras durch blutigem
Dienst, und geschlachtete Menschen mussten zu
Extispicien dienen.[4] Nach Hadrianus setze man
ihn wieder fort, und der Kaiser Commodus opferte dem Mithras eigenhändig einen Menschen."[5]
Of the German writers on Roman History,
Mommsen deserves particular attention.[6] " At
the very core of the Latin religion there lay that
profound moral impulse which leads men to bring
earthly guilt and earthly punishment into relation
with the world of the gods and to view the former

---

[1] Vol. ii.
[2] Porphyr., *De Abstin. Carnis*, ii. 56 ; Clem. Alex., *Protrep*,
c. 3, *init.;* Lact., *Instit.*, i. 21.
[3] Bei'm Porphyrius, ii., p. 282, ed. Rhoer.
[4] Photti. Bibl., p. 1446, Socrates, *Histor. Eccles.*, iii. 2.
[5] Lamprid., cap. 19.   [6] Vol. i., pp. 232, 233.

as a crime against the gods and the latter as its expiation. The execution of the criminal condemned to death was as much an expiatory sacrifice offered to the divinity as the killing of an enemy in just war. The thief who by night stole the fruits of the field, paid the penalty to Ceres on the gallows, just as the enemy paid it to mother earth and the good spirits on the field of battle. The profound and fearful idea of substitution also meets us here. When the gods of the community were angry and nobody could be laid hold of as definitely guilty, they might be appeased by one who voluntarily gave himself up (devovere se). Noxious chasms in the ground were closed, and battles half lost were converted into victories, when a brave burgess threw himself as an expiatory offering into the abyss or upon the foe. The " sacred spring," was based on a similar view : all the offspring, whether of cattle or of men, within a specified period were presented to the gods.

" If acts of this nature are to be called human sacrifices, then such sacrifices belonged to the essence of the Latin faith ; but we are bound to add that, so far back as our view reaches into the past, this immolation, so far as life was concerned, was limited to the guilty who had been convicted before a civil tribunal, or to the innocent who voluntarily chose to die. Human sacrifices of a different description, which are inconsistent with the fundamental idea of a sacrificial act, and which, wheresoever they have occurred, among the Indo-Germanic stocks at least, have been the offspring of later degeneracy and barbarism, never gained admission among the Romans ; hardly in a single instance were superstition and despair induced even in times of extreme distress to seek an extraordinary deliverance through means so revolting."

It will be observed that Mommsen, on the one hand, most fully recognizes the fact of human sacrifices among the Romans in even greater frequency than other writers. But on the other hand, while stating strongly the instinct and idea which more or less consciously lead to expiatory sacrifices, he yet so ennobles the action of this instinct and idea in " the Latin religion," as considerably to qualify the fact itself, and by a certain German largeness of expression vindicates the Romans from sacrificing any but those " convicted before a civil tribunal, or the innocent who voluntarily chose to die." How much the Latin religion preserved of " the profound moral impulse " which Mommsen ascribes to it, and how far and intelligently the Romans with their inheritance of the dark Etruscan, were moved by it, is a question which deserves very serious consideration before admitting the full statement we have quoted. Meanwhile it rests with every student to examine the instances recorded of the sacrifices themselves.

Niebuhr [1] writes of the taking of Perusia by

[1] Vol. ii., p. 107.

Octavius: "three hundred of the most distinguished citizens of the town were afterwards solemnly sacrificed at the altar of Julius Divus." And this without any question of the fact.

Of English authors on Rome, Gibbon, in remarking upon M. de Fontenelle's criticism of the Romans' prohibition of human sacrifices by the Carthaginians, writes :[1] " M. de Fontenelle is pleased to accuse the Romans of contradicting their own practice, since they sacrificed a man every year to Jupiter Latialis. But I shall not believe upon the words of only Porphyry, Lactantius, and Prudentius, that human sacrifices were ever a regular part of the Roman worship." But the question is not of the extent to which human sacrifices prevailed among the Romans; to determine that is indeed difficult and not now attempted. The sacrifice to Jupiter Latialis, wholly denied by Macaulay in view of the testimony of Lactantius and Porphyry, and not believed as proving " human sacrifices " to be a regular part of the Roman worship " by Gibbon on the words of Lactantius, Porphyry, and Prudentius, will be found to be mentioned by others besides the three authors just named. Arnold[2] records " the first exhibition of gladiators ever known at Rome. . . . . The spectacle from the very beginning excited the liveliest interest at Rome, but for many years it was exhibited only at

[1] *Index Expurg., Miscell. Works*, v. 563.   [2] Vol. ii., pp. 134-5.

funerals, as an offering in honor of the dead ; the still deeper wickedness of making it a mere sport, and introducing the sufferings and death of human beings as a luxury for the spectators in their seasons of the greatest enjoyment, was reserved for a later period." On page 263 of vol. ii., he also records the burial in the Forum Boarium of a man and woman of the Gaulish race alive, with a Greek man and woman.

On the subject of human sacrifices, Merivale [1] writes : " Laxity of principle and indifference of belief had their attractions for the vulgar, while the nobler lessons of philosophy, its ideas of equity and natural right, would only be appreciated by the refined and educated. The priests, who belonged to this latter class, might shrink from the atrocity of human sacrifices and extenuate the literal signification of the most of the national dogmas ; the nobles might soften the rigor of ancient law; but to the common people, these silent changes were offensive or unintelligible. The literature of Rome, adopted as it was from Greece, was an instrument for enlarging men's ideas and refining their sentiments; but it remained a dead letter to the mass of the citizens, to whom the glowing spectacles of the circus and amphitheatre proved more attractive than the intellectual culture of a conquered foe." In a note on the same page, he writes, " The Romans af-

[1] Vol. ii., p. 416.

firmed that human sacrifices had been abolished by the elder Brutus.[1] But on three occasions, at least, such victims were demanded at a much later period; namely, in the year u. c. 527,[2] and again u. c. 536;[3] and once more u. c. 640.[4] Soon after this the rite was denounced by a decree of the Senate A. U. C. 657.[5] But compare[6] 'Boario vero in foro Græcum Græcamque defossos, aut aliarum gentium cum quibus res esset, etiam nostra ætas vidit.' Dion Cassius, indeed, asserts that a sacrifice of this kind took place at the triumph of Julius Cæsar,[7] and adds that he can not find that any oracle required it. The statements of the Greeks on any subject of this kind are to be received with caution, both on account of their ignorance of Roman manners and their prejudice against them. Thus Eusebius[8] affirms that human sacrifices were continued at Rome to his day, alluding perhaps to the words of Lactantius:[9] 'Etiam nunc sanguine colitur humano Jupiter Latiaris,' which undoubtedly refers only to a libation of the blood of gladiators. Dion's statement may be some misconception of the nature of a military punishment. In ancient times the consul, prætor, or dictator could devote to Mars a victim

---

[1] Macrob., i. 7. [2] Oros., iv. 13.
[3] Liv., xx. 57; minime Romano sacro.
[4] Plut., *Qu. Rom.*, p. 284. [5] Plin., *H. N.*, xxx. 3.
[6] xxviii. 3. [7] xliii. 24.
[8] *Paneg.*, 13. [9] *De Falsa Rel.*, i. 21.

selected from the legion.[1]   The story of the human sacrifices of Octavius at the capture of Perusia,[2] is dubious and obscure."

On this text and note of Merivale it may be
remarked that he evidently wavers in his judgment. Of his comments on Dion, Lactantius,
and Suetonius others must judge. Merivale's
opinion is worthy of respect, but any testimony
can be explained away in this manner. Sir G. C.
Lewis does not thus discredit Dion Cassius, but in
a note on page 430, 2d volume of his " Credibility of Roman History," writes: " Two men were
slain as victims by the Pontifices and the priest
of Mars, in the Campus Martius, and their heads
were affixed to the Regia in the year 46 B. C.,
under the rule of Julius Cæsar. Dion Cassius
states that he does not know the reason why this
sacrifice took place ; it was not made in conse-
quence of a sybilline oracle, or any other sacred
announcement."[3]   The opinion of the author of
the article in Smith's " Greek and Roman Antiquities " is worthy of attention. He writes in
reference to the instance given by Dion: " One
awful instance is known which belongs to the latest period of the Roman republic."[4]   In the article " Funus " from the same work, speaking of the
obsequies, the writer remarks : " Sometimes animals were slaughtered at the pile, and in ancient

---

[1] Liv., viii. 10.

[2] Suetonius, *Octav.*, 15.

[3] xliii. 24.

[4] Dion Cassius, xliii. 24.

times captives and slaves, since the Manes were
supposed to be fond of blood; but afterwards
gladiators, called Bustuarii, were hired to fight
round the burning pile." [1] We close the list of
English authors accessible by referring to Magee
on " The Atonement," [2] who enumerates the nations offering human sacrifices, and cites some of
the ancient authors already mentioned in proof of
the practice being preserved by the Romans to a
late period. Also to Thomson's " Bampton Lec-
tures " [3] where after reference to the three hundred and seven Roman prisoners immolated by
the Etruscan Tarquinii," [4] to " the sacrifice of human victims in any great and general calamity,
by order of the books of fate, with magical forms
of prayer repeated by the president of the College of Fifteen who had charge of the Sybilline
Books," [5] to " the decree forbidding human sacrifices, not issued till the year 657 of the city, or 97
before Christ,[6] the author confidently quotes Dion
Cassius in the instance not credited by Merivale; [7]
then without question refers to the sacrifice at Perusia by Augustus,[8] next the voluntary sacrifice
of the beautiful Antinous for the Emperor, [9] and

[1] Serv., *Ad Virg.*, x. 519 ; comp. Hor., *Sat.*, ii. 3, 85.
[2] Vol. i., 88–109.   [3] Lect. ii. ; note 26, p. 38.
[4] Liv., vii. 15.
[5] Plin., xxviii. 2, 12 ; Liv., xxii. 57 ; Plut., *Marcel.*, p. 299 ; *C. et Mor.*, p. 283.
[6] Plin., xxx. 1, 12.   [7] Dion Cassius, xliii. 24.
[8] Dion Cassius, xlviii. 14 ; Suet., *Oct.*, 15 ; Seneca, *De Clem.*, i. 11.
[9] Xiphilinus, p. 356–21 ; Sylb., *Æl. Spartianus Hadriano*, 14 ;
Aur., *Victor de Cesar*, 14.

finally the annual immolation of men to Jupiter Latialis — as said to have continued even into the third century of our era.[1] In a French work — "Cerémonies et Coutumes Religieuses," supplement to a larger work, written in a state of mind philosophically inclined, as became 1783 in France, not to treat heathenism with undue severity in comparison with Christianity — we read : [2] " Il seroit bien difficile de déterminer l'époque où l'on cessa d'immoler des victimes humaines à Rome. Quoique les empereurs et le sénat eussent porté plusieurs édits et sénatus consultes, pour abolir cette pratique dans toute l'étendue de leur empire, elle ne laissa pas de subsister sous leurs yeux ; puis qu'il est certain qu'on enterra encore vivans dans le marché aux bœufs, au rapport de Pline et Grec et une Grecque, l'an 830, de la fondation de Rome, qui tombe à la fin du regne de Vespasien. On sait que le furieux Heliogabale, ayant bâti dans Rome un temple dont il avoit été consacré prêtre, avant son elevation à l'empire lui sacrifoit les plus beaux enfans qu'il pouvoit trouver en Italie ; et que pendant que les magiciens immolaient ces jeunes victimes, il faisoit ses prieres à son idole, et regardoit lui meme les

---

[1] Porphyr., *De Abst.*, 2, 56 ; Justin Martyr, *Apol.*, 2, p. 100 D; Theophilus, *Ad Autol.*, iii., p. 412 E ; Tatian, *Adv. Græcos*, p. 284 B ; Euseb., *De Laud. Constant.*, xiii. 5, 1198 : Zimmerm., *Tertul. Apol.*, 8, and Scorp., *Adv. Gnost.*, vii. ; Minuc. Fel., *Octav.*, xxi. 15, xxx. 4 ; Lactant., i. 21, 30; Prudent., *Adv. Symmach.*, i. 380.
[2] Vol. iv. p. 156.

entrailles des hosties, pour y remarquer les pré-
sages de ses prospérités.[1] On lit même dans l'his-
toire que l'empereur Aurélien, qui régnoit sur
les Romains, au milieu du quatrieme siecle, c'est-
à-dire, plus de cent ans après Heliogabale, ayant
écrit au sénat, pour le prier de consulter les livres
Sybillins offrit de fournir pour les sacrifices des
prisonniers de telle qu'on le jugeroit à propos, si
l'oracle l'ordonnoit." Then, after some reflections
on a superstition like this being so strangely
shared in by such distinguished people as a Roman senate, and after soothing the philosophic
mind by the conjecture that doubtless all but
a "tres petit nombre" in "that august body"
mocked in secret at the public credulity — the
author proceeds: "Mais les guerres continuelles
que le peuples Romain avoient essuyées depuis
sa naissance, les nombreux combats de gladia-
teurs, qui formoiént son spectacle journalier,
avoient tellement endurci le cœur de ces republi-
cains, que la vie de quelques misérables etrangers
pris en guerre et sur lesquels, par conséquent,
selon la coutume absurde qui régnoit alors, ils
croyoient avoir le droit de vie et de mort; ne
leur paroissoit pas d'une assez grande importance,
pour faire cesser des usages que leur religion
avoit anciennement consacrés." On page 129,
vol. iv., the same work contains the following on
the Gladiatorial combats. "Tout ce qui distin-

---

[1] Lamprid. in Heliogab.

guoit ces sacrifices de ceux que faisoient les autres nations, consistoit en ce que, chez celles-ci,
les particuliers qui offroient ces victimes et les
prêtres qui les égorgeoient sur les autels our sur
les tombeaux, se rendoient seuls coupables de ce
crime: au lieu qu'a Rome, toute la république
tranquille et froide spectatrice des combats qui
se livroient dans l'arene, devoit être réputée com-
plice des meurtres qui s'y commettoient. On
sait que cet usage, introduit dans la république
Romaine, par Junius Brutus, qui honora les
mânes de son pere par la mort de plusieurs de ces
malheureux, fut substitué à la coutume qu'on y
pratiquoit, au rapport de Servius et de Tertul-
lien, d'immoler des prisonniers de guerre ou
toutes autres victimes, par ceux dès citoyens qui
avoient le moyen de se les procurer. Cette inno-
cence au lieu d'arrêter les fleuves de sang qui
couloient aux funérailles, ne fit que donner un
nouvel aliment à la barbarie romaine."

In Montfauçons "Antiquities," translated by
Humphreys,[1] after speaking of the sacrifice of
captives to the manes of the deceased, the author
proceeds : " But this seems to be but rarely used,
because, as Servius acquaints us, the Romans
thought it too cruel, and changed it for another
which was but a very little less barbarous. They
obliged Gladiators to fight at the Pile. — These
Gladiators were called Bustuarii, from Bustum,

which signifies the Place where the dead Bodies
are burned. They poured some of the Blood
of these wretches on the Obolus which was in
the Mouth of the deceased." Montfauçon[1] does
not question the instance of " Marius, a Roman,
who also sacrificed his Daughter to the Gods
called Averrunci." It may be also well to cite
a modern French writer on the same question,
Champagny, who in a work entitled " Tableau du
Monde Romain sous les Premiers Empereurs,"
discusses the moral state of Rome. In all re-
spects his conclusions, severely drawn from the
nearest sources, are fearful to contemplate; but
not the least so are those regarding Rome's religion.[2] " Rome, il est vrai, après avoir versé tant de
sang par la guerre, avait eu horreur du sang des
sacrifices; elles avait pretendu faire cesser dans
tout l'univers les immolations. En effet, ces in-
fâmes sacrifices avaient cesse d'etre pratiqués pub-
liquement: mais il est trop certain qu'ils se con-
tinuaient en secret." Then after mentioning Gaul,
Laodicea, Africa, and even Greece, as places where
human sacrifices continued, he proceeds, " Rome,
d'aillurs, était elle bien en droit de sévir contre
ces crimes provinciaux? Ses combats de gladia-
teurs etaient ils autre chose, dans l'origine, que
des expiations religieuses? Rome, cette miseri-
cordieuse, Rome civilisée par la Gréce, courait aux
mystères de Bacchus que souillait l'effusion du

---

[1] In vol. ii., p. 95.   [2] Vol. iii., pp. 279, 280.

sang humain. Rome au temps même des Empereurs, n'avait pas abandonné la coutume, dans les jours de grande calamité, d'enterrer vivants, en un lieu marqué du Forum, un homme et une femme de race ennemie." To the above the writer adds in notes, " Sénatus consulte contre les sacrifices, en 656.[1] Ce qui n'empêche pas Porphyre de placer la cessation des sacrifices humain's au temps d'Hadrien seulement, c'est-à-dire, plus de cinquante ans apres Pline Porphyre[2] convient, du reste, qu'il s'en faisait encore de son temps; on faisait périr des esclaves, non seulement à titre de punition ou pour des opérations magíques, mais même à titre de sacrifice.[3]

From a work by Joann. Saubertus[4] in 1699, we make the following extracts:[5] " Adéo exsecramur Heliogabali inhumanitatem, cædentis humanas hostias, lectis ad hoc pueris nobilibus et decoris per omnem Italiam, patrimis et matrimis, ut major esset utrique parenti dolor."[6] On p. 458, in same chapter, the author quotes Sueton. Octav. 15, before referred to, without question of its credibility. So on p. 460 he writes: " Jupiter Latialis sanguine humanô ex hostiis sibi cæsis proluebatur testibus Athanasiô et Tertulliano." Then again, on p. 462, he records the testimony of Minucius Felix,

[1] Pliny, *Hist. Nat.*, xxx., 1 ; Paul. V., *Sentent.*, xxiii. 16.
[2] *De Abstinentiâ Carnis*, ii. 56.
[3] Juvenal, v. 551 ; xii. 115.   [4] *De Sacrific. Veter.*
[5] Cap. xxi., 455–56.   [6] Lampr. in ejus *Vit.*, c. viii.

to the last-mentioned sacrifice. On the subject
of gladiatorial contests, Græv., " Thesaur. Ant.
Rom.," [1] has the following: " Obolo incluso primis
temporibus effundebatur sanguis vel captivorum
vel gladiatorum. [2] Olim quoniam animas defunc-
tarum humano sanguine propitiari, creditum erat,
captivos vel magno ingenio servos mercati in
exsequis immolabant. . . . . Valer. Maximus ad-
notavit, gladiatorum munus primum (inquit) Romæ
datum est in Foro Boario, P. Claud. et M. Fulv.
Coss. Dederunt M. et D. Brute funebre memoria
patres cineres honorando." Lipsius should be an
authority on this question, and in his " De Am-
phiatr.," cap. iv., he quotes Tertullian and Prudentius and Minutius, in proof of the sacrificial
design of the gladiatorial contests. But of these
earlier modern writers none is so exhaustive upon
the subject as Jacobus Geussius [3] who, in 1675,
published at Groningen a work entire upon Human Sacrifices. The justness of some of his
conclusions from the authors he examines may
be disputed, but it is impossible to avoid the evidence which he has accumulated from antiquity
to show the universal prevalence of this cruel
worship. On the question of its early origin and
late continuance among the Romans, he has recorded numerous instances. Thus after [4] speak-

---

[1] Vol. xi., p. 1431–2, D, E, F.
[2] Dux et Auctor rei Tertullianus apud Lipsum.
[3] *Theol. et Med. Frisu.*   [4] Second Part, p. 136.

ing of sacrifice by fire as practiced by others, he says : " Nec ipsi Romani in hoc ritu fuerunt hospites et asymboli, nam in urbe Roma L. Furio et Serrana Consulibus puer auruspicum jussu crematus est. Sicut docet Iulius, Obsequens de Prodig., et, cum bellum civile — inter Cæsarem et Pompeium instaret, Romæ monstrosi partus combusti sunt ut ita urbs expiaretur et lustraretur."[1] In Part I., cap. xviii. and xix., when treating of bloody rites used in consecrations, auspices, and incantations, by different nations, he finds various illustrations in Roman history. Thus he quotes Plutarch,[2] for an instance in early times of an oath of conspiracy sealed in the blood of a human victim ; then, for later illustration, the fearful sacrament in Cataline's conspiracy, as mentioned by Dion, Sallust, Florus, and others. He gives Cicero himself as authority, when, writing of incantations, he adds : " Vatinium juxta fidem et exprobationem Ciceronis puerorum immolatorum exta Diis manibus ad magiam exercendam obtulisse." He even cites Horace in illustration, from an Epode not usually regarded as bearing this meaning of sacrifice, and introduces extracts from it with these words: " Quippe Canidia aliæque veneficæ ad poculum amatorium conficiendum medulla et jecinore pueri prætextati uti et abuti incubuerunt

---

[1] Lucan, lib. i., p. 29.　　　　[2] *Vita Poplic*, p. 98.

teste."[1] To show that human sacrifices were associated with divination and taking auspices, he refers to an accusation against Apollonius Tyaneus thus:[2] "Sic Domitianus Cæsar celebrem, illum Magum Apollonium Tyaneum insimulavit, quod in magicis suis sacris puerum immolasset,[3] Rursus."[4] Whether the charge were well founded or not, it shows the familiarity of the ancient mind with the practice. So in giving an illustration from Juvenal,[5] Geussius adds: "Videmus igitur ex Juvenale et ejus ætate hoc infanticidium et extispicium apud Romanos nondum æruginem contraxisse et obsolevisse." For later instances of the same he refers to "Maxentius Tyrannus," on authority of Eusebius,[6] and Joh. Zonaras, and to other Emperors.

These are some of the authors who have written at all on the subject of Human Sacrifices among the Romans, and their opinions may help us to form a judgment. But it may be a more complete argument to consider in order of time some of the passages from ancient authors referred to above. There can be no dispute about the existence of human sacrifices in the earliest times of Rome. The Etruscans, who are believed to have had no small share in the Roman religion,

---

[1] Horatio, Epode v., p. 120, 121. [2] *I. P.*, ch. xxi., p. 333.
[3] *Apud Philostrat.*, lib. vii., cap. 2.
[4] *Apud eundem Philostrat.*, lib. vii., cap. 10.
[5] Satyr vi., p. 54. [6] *Eccles. Hist.*, lib. viii., cap. 15, p. 99.

show on their monuments that they sacrificed human victims.[1] This is evident too from the continuance of rites which implied something substituted for living beings. Then, too, the decree against the practice of which Cicero and Pliny speak, of course proves its existence till then.

The first instance of human sacrifices mentioned by Livy occurs in lib. vii. 15, where it is related of the Tarquienses, a cognate Latin race, in u. c. 397, A. c. 355 : "Nec in acie tantum ibi cladis acceptum, quam quod trecentos septem milites Romanos captos Tarquinienses immolarunt." In the edition by "Twiss," is the following note on this passage : "Haud inusitato Etruscorum more si a sarcaphago ap. Tarquinios nuper effosso argumentum ducendum sit, quippe in eo humanis hostiis manes cujusdam ducis Etrusci placari cernimus."[2]

In lib. viii. 15, we have a minute account of the consul Decius devoting himself, u. c. 415, A. c. 337. "Deorum', inquit, ope, valeri opus est. Agedum pontifex publicus populi Romani, præi verba quibus me pro legionibus devoveam." Then, after a prayer of consecration and execration to the various gods, and, among others, to the "Divi novensiles" (the nine Gods of the Etruscans presiding over thunder and lightning according to Niebuhr): "Ipse, incinctus cinctu Gabinio armatus in equum insiluit, ac se in medios hostes immisit. Conspec-

---

[1] Vid. Dennis.　　　[2] Cf. Schueigh, *Ad Appion*, i. 117.

tus ab utraque acie aliquanto augustior humano visu, sicut cœlo missus piaculum omnis deorum iræ qui pestem ab suis aversam in hostes ferret." What follows in cap. 10 shows familiarity with propitiatory human sacrifices : " Illud adjiciendum videtur, licere consuli dictatorique et prætori, quum legiones hostium devoveat, non utique se, sed quem velit ex legione Romana Scripta civem, devovere : si is homo, qui devotus est, moritur, probe factum videri : ni moritur, tum signum septem pedes altum, aut majus, in terram defodi, et piaculum hostiam cædi. Ubi illud signum defossum erit, eo magistratum Romanum escendere fas non esse. Sin autem sese devovere volet, sicuti Decius devovit : ni moritur, neque suum, neque publicum divinum pure faciet, qui sese devoverit. Vulcano arma sive cui alii divo vovere volet, sive hostia sive quo alio volet, jus est. Telo, super quod stans consul precatus est, hostem potire, fas non est : si, potiatur, Marti suovetaurilibus piaculum fieri." True, he adds : " Hæc, etsi omnis divini humanique moris memoria abolevit, nova peregrinaque omnia priscis ac patriis præferendo, haud ab re duxi, verbis quoque ipsis, ut tradita nuncupataque sunt, referre." But the record remains. Later on[1] we have an account of a similar act of devotion by a son of Decius, attended by prayers and imprecations. In lib. xxii. 57, we find the instance so frequently referred to (u. c.

[1] Lib. x. 28.

7

536, A. C. 216): "Interim ex fatalibus libris sacrificia aliquot extraordinaria facta : inter quæ Gallus et Galla, Græcus et Græca, in foro boario subterra vivi demissi sunt in locum saxo consæptum, jam ante hostiis humanis, minime Romano sacro, imbutum." Here, too, is the comment "minime Romano sacro;" but the fact remains on record, and as we shall see, is fully admitted by other writers. On this passage the Oxford editor has a note by Gron. "Anno ante hunc undecimo ad idem scelus, quo jam imbutum hunc locum scribit Livius prava religio Romanos impulerat." Later than these dates we find the nobler Romans expressing disapprobation of these sacrifices. Thus Cicero in his oration,[1] speaking of other nations, says : "Quis enim ignorat, eos usque ad hunc diem retinere illam immanem ac barbaram consuetudinem hominum immolandorum ?" Pliny, too, claims for the Romans great praise that they prohibited this custom:[2] "DCLVII demum anno Urbis, Cn. Cornelio Lentulo, P. Licinio Crasso Coss., senatus consultum factum est, ne homo immolaretur." "Nec satis estimari potest, quantum Romanis debeatur qui sustulere monstra, in quibus hominem accidere religiosissimum erat, mandi vero etiam saluberrimum." This is what we might have expected from such men. So, too, they felt about other parts of paganism, and yet these continued. So, too, when Roman society grew

_____
[1] *Pro Fonteio*, xi. 21.   [2] Lib. xxx. 3, 4.

corrupt beyond description, there were found men
whose writings were in profound contrast with the
vileness about them, and still human sacrifices did
not cease. Cicero himself is witness to this. In
his " Orat. in Vatinium "[1] he thus inveighs against
a public officer: "Quæ te tanta pravitas mentis
tenuerit, qui tantus furor, ut, quum inaudita ac
nefaria sacra susceperis, quum inferorum animas
elicere, quum puerorum extis Deos manes mactare soleas; auspicia, quibus hæc urbs condita
est, quibus omnis respublica atque imperium ten-
etur, contempseris? initio que Tribunatus tui
Senatui denuntiaris, tuis actionibus augurum responsa atque ejus collegii arrogantiam impedi-
mento non futuram." Here is the strongest disapprobation ; here is the assertion that this particular use of human victims was in contempt of
the regular national auspices ; but here, too, is
published the actual employment of such means
of necromancy and the absence of any hindrance,

What Dionysius of Halicarnassus has written
on human sacrifices among the Romans may be
fitly introduced here. In " Antiq. Rom.,"[2] after
speaking of the ancient sacrifices of human beings
to Saturn, said to have been abolished by Hercules,
he describes how the ancient rite was changed by
the substitution of images thrown into the Tiber:
Ἵνα δὴ τὸ τῆς ὀττείας ὅ,τι δή ποτε ἦν ἐν ταῖς ἁπάν-

---

[1] vi. 14.   [2] Lib. i. 38.

τῶν ψυχαῖς παραμένον ἐξαιρεθῇ, τῶν εἰκόνων τοῦ παλαιοῦ ἔθους¹ ἔτι σωζομένων.² Then he adds : Τοῦτο δὲ καὶ μέχρις ἐμοῦ διετέλουν Ῥωμαῖοι δρῶντες ὅσον τὶ μικρὸν ὕστερον ἐαρινῆς ἰσημερίας, ἐν μηνὶ Μαΐῳ ταῖς καλουμέναις ἰδοῖς, διχομηνίδα βουλόμενοι ταύτην εἶναι τὴν ἡμέραν.³ Again, in lib. ii., x., after writing of certain sacred obligations, the author proceeds : —

Κοινῇ δ' ἀμφοτέροις οὔτε ὅσιον οὔτε θέμις ἦν κατηγορεῖν ἀλλήλων ἐπὶ δίκαις, ἢ καταμαρτυρεῖν, ἢ ψῆφον ἐναντίαν ἐπιφέρειν, ἢ μετὰ τῶν ἐχθρῶν ἐξετάζεσθαι. Εἰ δέ τις ἐξελεγχθείη τούτων τι δυαπραττόμενος, ἔνοχος ἦν τῷ νόμῳ τῆς προδοσίας, ὃν ἐκύρωσεν ὁ Ῥωμύλος. Τὸν δὲ ἁλόντα τῷ βουλομένῳ κτείνειν ὅσιον ἦν ὡς θῦμα τοῦ καταχθονίου Διός. Ἔθος γὰρ Ῥωμαίοις, ὅσους ἐβούλοντο νηποινὶ τεθνάναι, τὰ τούτων σώματα θεῶν ὅτῳ δή τινι, μάλιστα δὲ τοῖς καταχθονίοις κατονομάζειν ὁ καὶ τότε ὁ Ῥωμύλος ἐποίησε.⁴

¹ Vat. and Euseb., πάθους.

² "In order to remove whatever religious scruple still lingered in the minds of any, since he preserved images which represented the ancient usage."

⁸ "And until the present time the Romans have been in the habit of doing this, a little later than the vernal equinox, in the month of May, on the so-called Ides, regarding this day as the middle of the month."

⁴ "Both (parties) in common regarded it as neither pious nor right for the one to make a legal accusation against the other, or to bear witness against him, or to be reckoned among his enemies. If any one had been detected doing anything of this kind, he was liable to the law (for the punishment) of treason, which Romulus had sanctioned. And it was a pious act for any one who desired to slay a person convicted of this crime, as a sacrifice to the god of the lower world. For it was a custom of the Romans, if they wished to slay persons with impunity, to devote the bodies of such persons to some god, especially to those of the lower world, which Romulus did even at that time."

The instance recorded by Sallust, and referred to by other authors, is familiar to all, but may well be recalled here:[1] "Fuere ea tempestate, qui dicerent, Catalinam oratione habita, quum ad jusjurandum populares sceleris sui adigeret, humani corporis sanguinem vino permixtum in pateris circumtulisse, inde quum post exsecrationem omnes degustavissent sicuti in solemnibus sacris fieri consuerit, aperiusse consilium suum: atque eo dictitare fecisse, quo inter se magis fidi forent, alius alii tanti facinoris conscii." So far we have Sallust's account of the report." Then he adds: "Nonnulli ficta hæc, et multa præterea existumabant ab iis, qui Ciceronis invidiam, qui postea orta est, leniri credebant atrocitate sceleris eorum, qui pœnas dederant. Nobis ea res pro magnitudine parum comperta est."

But this added comment comes from a voluptuary who hated Cicero, and yet who has himself in undying words recorded the character of men and times in perfect harmony with such an act of bloody superstition. Besides, as we shall see, it was related by others who had no such feelings.

On Virgil,[2] Servius comments: "Apud veteres, etiam homines interficiebantur: sed mortuo Junio Bruto, cum multæ gentes ad ejus funus captivos mississent: nepos illius eos, qui missi erant inter

---

[1] C. C. Sallust, *De Conjurat. Catalin., Histor.*, xxii.
[2] *Æneid*, iii. 67.

se composuit et sic pugnaverunt et muneri missi
erant unde munus appellatum."

Upon the passage,[1] —

> " Sulmone creatos
> Quatuor hic juvenes : totidem quos educat Ufens.
> Viventes rapit, inferias quos immolet umbris, —
> Captivoque rogi perfundat sanguine flammas."

Heyne in a note remarks : " Nondum igitur ea
ætate metuendum fuit Maroni, ne displiceret im-
mane facinus lectoribus." The Epode in Horace,
which Geussius refers to as representing a human
sacrifice, is thus introduced by Anthon, one of the
editors of the poet. " A strange scene of magic
rites is introduced, and the piece opens with the
piteous exclamations of a boy of noble birth
whom Canidia and her associate hags are prepar-
ing to kill by a slow and dreadful process and
from whose marrow and dried liver a philter or
love-potion is to be prepared." The passage to
be particularly noted is,[2] —

> " Abacta nulla Veia conscientia
>   Ligonibus duris humum
>   Exhauriebat, ingemens laboribus ;
>   Quo posset infossus puer
>   Longo die bis terque mutatæ dapis
>   Inemori spectaculo
> Quum promineret ore, quantum exstant aqua
>   Suspensa mento corpora :
> Exsucca uti medulla et aridum jecur
>   Amoris esset poculum
> Interminato quum semel fixæ cibo
>   Intabuissent pupulæ."

Æneid, x. 517-520.   [2] Epode v. 29-40.

It is not a question if Horace had before him an actual occurrence. But in ridiculing " those females of the day, in whose licentious habits age had been able to produce no alteration, and who when their beauty had departed, had recourse to strange and superstitious expedients for securing admirers," he could not well have thus described a purely imaginary scene, but must have drawn the picture from magic rites existing then and familiar to his readers. The description in Lucan's " Pharsalia," [1] of the Thessalian sorceress whom Cn. Pompeius consults for the purpose of learning the future of the Civil War, is not unlike in its conception the fifth Epode of Horace. It is even more revolting in its details of horrors. Here is one passage : —

> " Nec cessante, cæde manus, si sanguine vivo
> Est opus, erumpat jugulo qui primus aperto."

The whole passage strengthens the conclusion that such bloody rites, though not public, were still practiced. The passage in Ovid [2] referred to by Prof. E. von Lasaulx as an instance of preserving the memory of human immolation, is as follows : —

> " Fama vetus : tum cum Saturnia terra vocata est
> Talia fatidici dicta fuere Dei :
> Falcifero libata seni duo corpora, gentes,
> Mittite ; quæ Tuscis excipiantur aquis.
> Donec in hæc venit Tithynthius arva quotannis
> Tristia Leucadio sacra peracta modo.

---

[1] Lib. vi. 554, 555.   [2] *Fast.*, lib. v. 621.

Illum Stramineos in aquam missise Quirites,
Herculis exemplo corpora falsa jaci,
Pars putat ut ferrent juvenes suffragia soli,
Pontibus infirmos præcipitasse senes."

Valerius Maximus, writing in the reign of Tiberius, thus speaks [1] of the gladiatorial spectacles :
" Nam gladiatorium munus primum Romæ datum
in foro Boario, Ap. Claudio. M. Fulvio consulibus ;
dederunt M. et D. Bruti, funebri memoria patris
cineres honorando."

In lib. ix., cap. vii., 2 : " Pro consule istud tam
violenter exercitus ; illud adversus consulem. Q.
enim Pompeium Syllæ Collegam, senatus jussu
ad exercitum Cn. Pompeii quem aliquamdiu in-
vita civitate obtinebat, contendere ausum, am-
bitiosi ducis illecebris corrupti milites, sacrificare
incipientem adorti, in modum hostiæ mactaverunt,
tantumque scelus curia, castris cedere se confessa,
inultum habuit."

The human sacrifice at Perusia has been ques-
tioned ; but Seneca, — whom rationalistic theolo-
gians delight to quote, and admirers of pagan mo-
rality love to exalt, and destructive historical critics
regard as authority — writes in his " De Clementia," [2] of Augustus, the cold dramatic Cæsar :
" Fuerit moderatus et clemens : nempe post
mare Actia cum Romano cruore infectum, nempe
post fractas in Siciliâ classes, et suas et alienas :
nempe post Perusinas aras et proscriptiones."

---

[1] Vol. i., lib. 2, cap. 4, sect. 7.   [2] Lib. i., sect. ii.

Lipsius' note on this is : " Ad quas trecenti è dedi-
tiicis, hostiarum more, mactati, Suetonius et Dio
qui tamen quadringentos." Seneca, too, in his
" De Ira,"[1] thus speaks of the atrocities of Rome's
domestic feuds on one occasion : " Quis erat hujus
imperii minister? Quis, nisi Catalina, jam in omne
facinus manus exercens? hic illum ante bustum
Q. Catuli carpebat, gravissimus mitissimi viri cine-
ribus; supra quos vir mali exempli, popularis tamen et non tam immerito quam nimis amatus, per
stillicidia sanguinem dabat." We have seen that
Pliny claimed much for the Romans[2] in forbidding human sacrifices. This was, according to
him, DCLVII. anno urbis. Yet in lib. xxviii.[3] he has
written : " Boario vero in foro Græcum Græcamque defossos, aut aliarum gentium, cum quibus
tum res esset, etiam nostra ætas vidit." Geussius,
when quoting Lucan and others for illustration of
human immolations in incantations, adds : " Idem
fortasse Plinius innuit.[4] Alii medullas crurum
quærunt, et cerebrum infantium." The passage
in lib. xxx. 6, referred to by Hen. Guil. Vent.,
when speaking of Nero, reads thus : " Nam homines immolare etiam gratissimum."

The poet Juvenal, as quoted by Geussius,[5] has
these lines : —

[1] Lib. iii., sect. 18.
[2] *Nat. Hist.*, lib. xxx. 4.
[3] *Nat. Hist.*, lib. xxviii. 11.
[4] Lib. xxx. 3.
[5] *Sat.*, vi. 571–76.

" Spondet amatorem tenerum, vel divitis orbi
Testamentum ingens, calidæ pulmone columbæ
Tractato, Armenius, vel Commagenus haruspex.
Pectora pullorum rimatur et exta Catelli,
Interdum pueri."

The reference to Juvenal by Champagny[1] : —

" Alter enim, si concedas mactare, vovebit
De grege servorum magna, et pulcherrima quæque
Corpora : vel pueris, et frontibus ancillarum
Imponet vittas : et si qua est nubilis illi
Iphigenia domi, dabit hanc altaribus etsi
Non sperat tragicæ furtiva piacula cervæ."

The instances of human immolation, already
referred to by different writers, in Suetonius,
are : [2] " Perusia Capta, in plurimos animadvertit,
orare veniam vel excusare se conantibus una voce
occurrens, moriendum esse. Scribunt quidam, trecentos ex dediticiis electos, utriusque ordinis, ad
aram Divo Julio exstructam Idibus Martiis hostiarum more mactatos." Earlier than Suetonius, Seneca, as we have seen in his " De Clementia," when
writing of Octavius Cæsar, refers to " Aras Perusinas " without questioning the fact. In " Vita
Tiberii," [3] there is mention of gladiatorial of-
ferings to the manes of kindred made by Tiberius. " Munus gladiatorum in memoriam patris, et
alterum in avi Drusi dedit — diversis temporibus
ac locis, primum in foro, secundum in amphithea-
tro." The references by Döllinger and Seppo are

---

[1] *Sat.*, xii. 115.   [2] *Vit. Octav.*, 15.
[3] *Sueton. Vita Tiberius*, vii.

the following : [1] " Alterum qui se periturum ea de causa voverat, cunctantem pueris tradidit : verbenatum infulatumque,[2] votum reposcentes, per vicos agerent, quoad præcipitaretur ex aggere. Multos honesti ordinis, deformatos prius stigmatum notis, ad metalla et munitiones viarum aut ad bestias condemnavit, aut bestiarum more quadrupedes cavea coërcuit, aut medios serra disseccuit."[3] "Stella crinita, quæ summis potestatibus exitium portendere vulgo putatur per continuas noctes oriri cœperat. Anxius ea re, ut ex Babilo astrologo didicit, solere reges talia ostenta cœde aliqua illustri expiare atque a semet in capita procerum depellere, — nobilissimo cuique exitium destinavit." The comment on this passage has been already given.

In the fragment remaining of Julius Obsequens' singular " Book of Prodigies," we find the following instance of human immolation by the "Aruspices : "[4] " Fulmine pleraque dejecta, puer aruspicum jussu crematus, cinisque ejus in mare dejectus." Annæus Florus, writing in the same period of literature in the time of Trajan, mentions repeatedly human sacrifices. Thus, in lib. i., cap. xvi. 7, giving the character of the Samnites, an Italian nation like the Romans, he says : " Pro hac urbe, his regionibus populus Romanus Samnites invasit, gentem, si opulentiam quæras,

---

[1] *Vit. Calig.*, 27.
[3] *Vit. Nero*, 36.
[2] " Adorned as a *victim*."
[4] Diviner.

aureis et argenteis armis, discolori veste, usque
ad ambitum armatam ; si fallaciam, saltibus fere
et montium grassantem : si rabiem ac furorem,
sacratis legibus, humanis que hostiis, in exitium
urbis agitatam : si pertinaciam, sexies rupto
fœdere, cladibusque ipsis animosiorem." In the
same Book[1] he narrates the self devotion of
Decius, recorded by Livy and others : " Nec
incruenta illa victoria, nam oppressus in sinu val-
lis alter consulum Decius, more patrio devotum
diis manibus obtulit caput : solennemque famil-
iæ consecrationem in victoriæ pretium redegit."
In lib. ii., 6, 8, we have the same idea : " Similis
exitus belli initio fuit.　Nam, quasi has inferias
sibi Saguntinorum ultimæ diræ in illo publico
parricidio incendiorum mandassent, ita Manibus
eorum vastatione Italiæ, captivitate Africæ, ducum
et regum, qui id gessere bellum, exitio parentatum
est."

In lib. iii., 18, 8 : " Primum fuit belli in Albano
monte consilium, ut festo die Latinarum, Julius
Cæsar et Martius Philippus consules, inter sacra
et aras immolarentur." This is found in the
chapter on the social war, and shows how familiar
was this idea of immolation.　The same book in
Florus, has a chapter on the Servile War, in
which [2] it is said : " Nec abnuit ille de stipen-
dario Thrace miles, de milite desertor, inde latro,
dein in honore virium gladiator qui defunctorum

[1]　Lib. i. 17, 6.　　　[2]　xx. 8-9.

quoque prælio ducum funera imperatoriis cele-
bravit exequiis, captivosque circa rogum jussit
armis depugnare, quasi plane expiaturus omne
præteritum dedecus, si de gladiatore munerator
fuisset."

We shall see this more fully brought out in another writer. Florus, when describing the Marian
civil war,[1] uses this language : " Tum Marius ju-
venis et Carbo consules, quasi desperata victoria,
ne inulti perirent, in antecessum sanguine Senatus
sibi parentabant obsessaque Curia, sic de Senatu,
quasi de carcere, qui jugularentur, educti." The
word " parentabant " shows the prevalence of at
least the notion of the bloody superstition under
review. In the chapter on the " Bellum Catili-
narium,"[2] this writer records without question the
dreadful sacrament described by Sallust : " Addi-
tum est pignus conjurationis sanguis humanus,
quem circumlatum pateris bibere."

From Appian, writing during the time of Trajan, we extract two instances of gladiatorial offer-
ings to the Manes. The first,[3] Καὶ τῆς ταφῆς
ἐκτελεσθείσης ἀγῶνα μονομάχων ἀνδρῶν ἤγαγον ἐπὶ
τοῦ τάφου,[4] was at the funeral of Viriathrus, the
Lusitanian general so long successful against the
Romans. The second,[5] Ὁ δὲ Σπάρταχος τρια-

---

[1] In lib. iii., 21, 20.　　　　　　　　　[2] Lib. iv. 1, 4.

[3] Βιβλος ζ, 75, Ιβηρικη.

[4] " And when the burial was completed, they held a contest of
single combatants (gladiators) on the grave."

[5] Ἐμφυλιων Βιβλ., Α' 117.

κοσίους Ῥωμαίων αἰχμαλώτους ἐναγίσας Κρίξῳ,[1] refers to an incident in the life of the famous
guerrilla chief whom the writer in Smith's "Classical Dictionary" praises so highly and at the
same time without question recognizes as the
offerer of this sacrifice, at this time in Roman
history. In this narration the word 'ἐναγίσας,'
like "parentavit" in the Latin translation of
Appian, cannot be mistaken. Plutarch has been
referred to. The following are instances in his
works where human sacrifices are mentioned.[2]
"*Quest.* 'What is the reason that the Romans
when they were informed that the barbarians
called Bletonesians had sacrificed a man to the
gods sent for their magistrates to punish them;
but when they made it appear that they did it in
obedience to a certain law they dismissed them,
but prohibited the like action for the future?
whenas (whereas?) they themselves not many
years preceding, buried two men and two women
alive in the Forum Boarium, two of whom were
Greeks and two Gauls?' *Solution:* 'What if this
be the reason : that they reckoned it profane to
sacrifice a man to the gods but necessary to do
so to the demons? Or were they of opinion that
they sinned that did such things by custom or
law; but as for themselves, they did it being

---

[1] " Spartacus having offered three hundred Roman captives to
Crixus."

[2] Transl. *Plutarch's Morals*, ed. Prof. Goodwin, vol. ii., *Rom.
Quest.*, 83.

enjoined to it by the Sibylline books. It was thought meet that the priest should consult the Sibylline books, where there were oracles found foretelling these things would come to pass for mischief to the republic, and enjoining them — in order to avert the impending calamity — to provide two Grecians and two Gauls, and bury them alive in that place, in order to the appeasing some alien and foreign demons."

After giving a Grecian story of human sacrifice, quoting Euripides " in his Erectheus," Plutarch proceeds with a Roman parallel : [1] "Marius, finding himself hard put to it in the Cimbrian war, had it revealed to him in a dream that he should overcome his enemies if he would but sacrifice his daughter Calpurnia. He did it, preferring the common safety before any private bond of nature, and he got the victory." For this Plutarch quotes Dorotheus in the fourth book of his " Italian History." In Clough's edition of " Plutarch's Lives," we have the immolation mentioned above in the " Rom. Quest.," again referred to. The " Life of Marcellus "[2] has this passage : " For though they were most averse to barbarous and cruel rites, and entertained more than any nation the same pious and reverent sentiments of the gods with the Greeks ; yet when this war was coming upon them, they then, from some prophecies in the Sibyl's books, put alive, underground,

[1] *Par. Rom. Græc.*, vol. v., 20.   [2] Vol. ii., p. 240.

a pair of Greeks, one male, the other female ; and likewise two Gauls, one of each sex, in the market called the Beast Market." So in the " Life of Cicero,"[1] we have the same incident recorded by Sallust respecting Cataline, and without any question of its truth : " This man, the profligate citizens choosing for their captain gave faith to one another, amongst other pledges, by sacrificing a man and eating of his flesh." There is a question about the time and person of Petronius (Arbiter); but it will not be amiss to quote from him in this place, for his descriptions and allusions belong to the empire. In " Satyric," cap. 1, we read : " Sed responsa in pestilentia data, ut virgines tres aut plures immolentur." Cap. 45 has the following : " Dedit gladiatores sestertiarios, jam decrepitos, quos si sufflasses cecidissent : jam meliores bestiarios vidi." Upon the word *bestiarios* Reines remarks : " Lege ' bustuarios ' qui ante sepulcra virorum illustrium placandis eorum manibus dimicabant die inferiarum." Again in " Satyric," cap. 121 : " Omnia, quæ tribui Romanis arcibus, odi : Muneribusque meis irascor : destruat istas Idem, qui posuit, moles Deus : et mihi cordi quippe cremare viros, et sanguine pascere luxum." Geussius' note on this passage is : " Ex quibus verbis apparet, quod ad gladiatores in funeribus exhibitos et Romæ immolatos respexerit."

[1] Vol. v., p. 45.

We now come where Christian and Pagan writers appear together, and we quote from them according to their time. Thus Justin Martyr distinctly recognizes the continuance of human sacrifices in his day. In his "First Apology"[1] we read: "For let even necromancy and the divinations you practice by immaculate children, etc., etc." Note by Editor: "Boys and girls, or even children prematurely taken from the womb, were slaughtered and their entrails inspected, in the belief that the souls of the victims (being still conscious, as Justin is arguing) would reveal things hidden and future. Instances are abundantly cited by Otto and Trollope."

In his "Second Apology"[2] we have the following: "For why did we not even publicly profess that these were the things which we esteemed good and prove that these are the divine philosophy, saying that the mysteries of Saturn are performed when we slay a man, and that when we drink our fill of blood, as it is said we do, we are doing what you are doing before that idol you honor, and on which you sprinkle the blood not only of irrational animals, but also of men, making a libation of the blood of the slain, by the hand of the most illustrious and noble man among you."

[1] Ch. 18, Translat., ed. Roberts and Donaldson: J. T. Clarke, Edinburgh.
[2] *Second Apol.*, chap. xii.

9

Another Christian writer, Tatian, writes:[1]—

" Wherefore having seen these things, and moreover also having been admitted to the mysteries, and having everywhere examined the religious rites performed by the effeminate and pathic, and having found among the Romans their Latiarian Jupiter delighting in human gore and the blood of slaughtered men, and Artemis not far from the great city sanctioning acts of the same kind, and one demon here and another there instigating to the perpetration of evil,— retiring by myself, I sought how I might be able to discover the truth." Another Father about the same time, Theophilus, in his book " To Autolycus,"[2] has the following : "For denying there are gods they again acknowledge their existence, and they said they committed grossly wicked deeds. For why should I recount the impurities of the so-called mother of the gods or of Jupiter Latiaris thirsting for human blood." Following the order of history we next quote from Dion Cassius. In Book xxxvii.[3] we have in the account of Cataline's conspiracy the incident of human sacrifice mentioned by other writers. He uses the expression, παῖδα γὰρ τινὰ καταθύσας.[4]

Again in Book xliii.[5] he gives an instance of public immolation : —

---

[1] *Address to the Greeks*, chap. xxix.
[2] Book iii., chap. viii.
[3] Page 43, D.
[4] " For having sacrificed a boy."
[5] Page 226, B.

Ἄλλοι δὲ δύο ἄνδρες ἐν τρόπῳ τινὶ ἱερουργίας ἐσφάγησαν, καὶ τὸ μὲν αἴτιον οὐκ ἔχω εἰπεῖν (οὔτε γὰρ ἡ Σιβύλλα ἔχρησεν οὔτ' ἄλλο τι τοιοῦτον λόγιον ἐγένετο) ἐν δὲ οὖν τῷ Ἀρείῳ πεδίῳ πρός τε τῶν ποντιφίκων καὶ πρὸς τοῦ ἱερέως τοῦ Ἄρεως ἐτύθησαν.[1]

In Book xlviii.,[2] Dion relates the Perusinian sacrifice offered by Augustus, which we have seen before in Seneca and Suetonius, with the difference of a somewhat larger number of victims.

Καὶ αὐτὸς μὲν, ἄλλοι τέ τινες ἄδειαν εὕροντο οἱ δὲ δὴ πλείους τῶν τε βουλευτῶν καὶ τῶν ἱππέων ἐφθάρησαν. Καὶ λόγος γε ἔχει ὅτι οὐδ' ἁπλῶς τοῦτο ἔπαθον, ἀλλ' ἐπὶ τὸν βωμὸν τὸν τῷ Καίσαρι τῷ προτέρῳ ὡσιωμένον ἀχθέντες ἱππεῖς τετρακόσιοι καὶ βουλευταὶ ἄλλοι τε καὶ ὁ Καννούτιος ὁ Τίτος (ὃς ποτε ἐν τῇ δημαρχίᾳ τὸ πλῆθος τῷ Καίσαρι τῷ Ὀκταουσιανῷ ἤθροισεν) ἐτύθησαν.[3]

The same book[4] describes offering of men in sacrifice to Neptune: —

Καὶ ὁ Σέξστος ἔτι καὶ μᾶλλον ἤρθη, καὶ τοῦ τε Ποσειδῶνος υἱὸς ὄντως ἐπίστευεν εἶναι, καὶ στολὴν κυανοειδῆ ἐνεδύσατο. Ἵππους τε (καὶ ὡς γέ τινές φασι) καὶ ἄνδρας ἐς τὸν πορθμὸν ζῶντας ἐνέβαλε.[5]

[1] "And two other men were slain in a certain manner of sacrifice; and I am not able to give the reason (for neither had the Sibyl so declared, nor was there any other oracle to this purport)· They were slain (ἐτύθησαν, sacrificed, geopfert; see Passow) therefore, in the Campus Martius by the pontiffs and the flamen of Mars."

[2] Page 365 C and D.

[3] "And he and certain others obtained amnesty, but the most of the senators and knights were put to death. And the report is current that they did not suffer death simply, but that three hundred knights and senators were slain, led like victims to the altar of the first Cæsar, and among the rest was Cannutius Tiberius (who once a plebeian tribune, had assembled the populace for Cæsar Octavianus).

[4] xlviii., p. 387 C.

[5] "And Sextus became yet more arrogant; and he believed that he

It is true, in giving the two instances of immolation last mentioned Dion writes λόγος γε ἔχει and τινές φασι; but even if he expresses nothing of his own view, his history records the occurrences as nothing strange to his readers.[1]

He records the death of Antinous with the evident belief that it was regarded as a sacrifice : Καὶ ἐν τῇ Αἰγύπτῳ ἐτελεύτησεν εἴτ᾽ οὖν εἰς τὸν Νεῖλον ἐκπεσὼν ὡς Ἀδριανὸς γράφει εἴτε καὶ ἱερουργηθεὶς ὡς ἡ ἀλήθεια ἔχει.[2]

Clement of Alexandria [3] refers to Dorotheus, the author quoted by Plutarch for the same statement, as relating the sacrifice of his daughter by Marius, then adds : " For a murder does not become a sacrifice by being committed in a particular spot. You are not to call it a sacred sacrifice if one slays a man either at the altar or on the highway to Artemis or Zeus, any more than if he slew him for anger or covetousness — other demons very like the former; but a sacrifice of this kind is murder and human butchery." Here certainly it is evident that the writer regarded human sacrifices as matter of fact in Roman heathenism.

In Cyprian's writings (same edition) is a treatise

was actually the son of Neptune, and put on a dark blue robe. Moreover, he cast alive into the strait, horses and (as some, at least, say) even men."

[1] Liber lxix., *Had.*, 793.

[2] "And he died in Egypt, whether he fell into the Nile, as Hadrian writes, or was sacrificed, as is the truth."

[3] Translat. *Ante-Nic. Lib.*, ed. Roberts and Donaldson, *Exhort. to the Heath.*, chap. 3.

on the Public Shows, by him or some unknown author, which contains the following: "What is the need of prosecuting the subject further, or of describing the unnatural kinds of sacrifices in the public shows, among which sometimes even a man becomes the victim by the fraud of the priest, when the gore, yet hot from the throat, is received in the foaming cup while it still steams, and, as if it were thrown into the face of the thirsty idol, is brutally drunk in pledge to it."

Minutius Felix in his "Octavius,"[1] is another witness to the bloody rites connected with the worship of Jupiter Latialis —"Quid ipse Jupiter vester? modo imberbis statuitur, modo barbatus locatur, et cum Hammon dicitur, habet cornua, cum Capitolinus, tunc gerit fulmina, et cum Latiaris, cruore perfunditur et cum Feretrius, tribus una aditur." Yet more plainly in sect. 30, after speaking of human sacrifices at other places and in other times, after mentioning the burying alive of the two Grecian and two Gallic victims in the Boarium Forum, so often noticed, he proceeds: "Hodieque ab ipsis Latiaris Jupiter homicidio colitur, et quod Saturni filio dignum, mali et noxii hominis sanguine saginatur." From Firmicus Maternus[2] we extract another reference to this sacrifice to Jupiter Latialis. It is part of the author's arraignment of Diabolus: " Nec venenis tuis cruor defuit nec semiustæ crematorum corpora partes

[1] 21.   [2] *De Errore Prof. Relig.*, 26.

humanarum te etiam victimarum frequenter sanguine cruentasti et Latiaris templi cruore vel ara
Carthagine rabies tua et siccarum faucium ve-
nena nutrita sunt."

None of the Latin Fathers has given more ex-
plicit testimony on the question of human sacrifices among the Romans than Tertullian ; thus the
passage on the Gladiatorial Games in one of his
Libr. Apol.[1] has been already referred to in the
extract from Lipsius, "De Amph." " Superest illius insignissimi spectaculi atque acceptissimi re-
cognitio. Munus dictum est ab officio, quoniam officium etiam muneris nomen est. Officium
autem mortuis hoc spectaculo facere se veteres
arbitrabantur posteaquam illud humaniore atrocitate temperaverunt. Nam olim quoniam animas
defunctorum humano sanguine propitiari creditum erat, captivos vel malo ingenio servos mercati
in exsequis immolabant. Postea placuit impie-
tatem voluptate adumbrare. Itaque quos parav-
erant armis, quibus tunc et qualiter poterant eru-
ditos, tantum ut occidi discerent, mox edicto die
inferiarum apud tumulos erogabant. Ita mortem
homocidiis consolobantur. Hæc muneris origo,
sed paulatim provecti ad tantam gratiam, ad quan-
tam et crudelilatem, quia ferrum voluptati satis
non faciebat, nisi et feris humana corpora dissipa-
rentur. Quod ergo mortuis litabatur, utique pa-
rentationi deputabatur."

[1] *De Spect.*, 12.

In his " Apol. adv. Gent." [1] he refers to the worship of Jupiter Latiaris: " Ecce in illa religiosissi-
ma urbe Æneadarum piorum est Jupiter quidam,
quem ludis suis humano proluunt sanguine. Sed
bestiarii, inquitis. Hoc, opinor, minus quam
hominis. An hoc turpius quod mali hominis?
Certe tamen de homicidio funditur." Again in
his " Contra Gnost. Scorp." [2] " Et Latio in hodier-
num Jovi media in urbe humanus sanguis ingus-
latur." Though, according to the inferences from
Tertullian's reply to some palliation offered, the
blood was from a Bestiarius, yet in itself and from
his understanding of the bloody shows of Rome,
he regarded the transaction as meaning human
sacrifice, for he is treating of that very subject.

We come now to Lactantius, of whom Macaulay
speaks somewhat contemptuously, as if his having
been a rhetorician unfitted him for truthful history.
Perhaps it did. Some critics judge the rhetorical
English historian in the same way. Nevertheless
other writers have a higher opinion of Lactantius.
Certainly his delineations of society and his descriptions of pagan morals are very life-like, besides
being confirmed abundantly from other sources.
The passage quoted by Gieseler and disposed of
so summarily by Macaulay is found in "Institut.
Div.," and reads thus: " Diximus de diis ipsis,
qui coluntur: nunc de sacris ac mysteriis eorum
pauca dicenda sunt. Apud Cyprios humanam

hostiam Jovi Teucrus immolavit: idque sacrificium posteris tradidit, quod est nuper, Hadriano imperante, sublatum. Erat lex apud Tauros, inhumanam et feram gentem, uti Dianæ hospites immolarentur: et id sacrificium multis temporibus celebratum. Galli esum atque Teutatem humano cruore placabant. Ne Latini quidem hujus immanitatis expertes fuerunt, siquidem Latialis Jupiter etiam nunc sanguine colitur." We have already seen that the criticism on "siquidem" would not stand, but in another part of his works Lactantius makes the same statement without "siquidem." In his "Div. Inst. Epit. ad Pentad.":[1] "Diximus de Diis nunc de ritibus sacrorum culturisque dicemus. Jovi Cyprio sicut Teucrus instituerat, humana hostia mactari solebat. Sic et Tauri Dianæ hospites immolabant. Latiaris quoque Jupiter humano sanguine propitiatus est." There can be no mistake about the meaning here. Lactantius writes of what existed at Rome in his day and was commonly known.

Still another allusion to this same offering is found in "Pontii Meropii Paulini Poem. Adv. Pagan."

> " Magnus uterque Deus ! Terris est abditus alter
> Alter non potuit terrarum scire latebras.
> Hinc Latiare malum prisci statuere Quirites
> Ut mactatus homo nomen satiaret inane."

In the " Hist. August. Script." we meet repeated

instances of human sacrifices. Thus in "Ælii
Spartiani Adrianus Cæsar,"[1] we find the story of
Antinous already referred to. "Antinoum suum
dum per Nilum navigat, perdidit, quem mulie-
briter flevit, de quo varia fama est, aliis eum devotum pro Hadriano asserentibus." Casaubon in
his notes on Spartianus remarks of this passage :
"Non dubitat Dio hoc affirmare, ut verum et cer-
tum ʹεἴτε δὲ ἱερουργηθεὶς ὡς ἡ ἀλήθεια ἔχει.ʹ Ob-
servabamus ad quartam Suetonii, veterum persua-
sionem hanc fuisse, posse alicujus produci fata,
si ejus vicem subiret alter, velut hostia quædam
succidanea."

In " Julii Capitolini M. Antonin. Philos.,"[2] we
have the brief notice of Marc. Antonin. and his
brother continuing the bloody rites of gladiatorial
combats at the grave: "Funebre munus patri
dederunt."

In " Ælii. Lampridii Antoninus Heliogabus,"[3]
we read: "Cædit et humanas hostias lectis ad hoc
pueris nobilibus et decoris per omnem Italiam patrimis et matrimis, credo ut major esse et utrique
parenti dolor. Omne denique magorum genus
aderat illi operabatur que quotidie, hortante illo
et gratias diis agente quod amicos corum invenis-
set, quum inspiceret exta puerilia et excuteret
hostias ad ritum gentilem suum."

The history by Jul. Capit. of Maximus and Bal-

---

[1] Page 7 C. [2] Page 25 D. [3] 103 E.

binus,[1] has the following : " His gestis, celebra-
tisque sacris, datis ludis scenicis ludisque circensi-
bus gladiatorio etiam munere, Maximus susceptis
votis in Capitolio, ad bellum contra Maximinum
missus est cum exercitio ingenti, prætorianis
Romæ manentibus. Unde autem mos tractus sit ut
proficiscentes ad bellum imperatores, munus gladiatorium et venatus darent, breviter dicendum est.
Multi dicunt, apud veteres hanc devotionem contra
hostes factam ut civium sanguine litato specie
pugnarum se Nemesis, id est vis quædam fortunæ,
satiaret. Alii hoc literis tradunt (quod verisimile
credo) ituros ad bellum Romanos debuisse pugnas
videre et vulnera et ferrum et nudas inter se co-
hortes, ne dimicantes in bello armatos hostes
timerent, aut vulnera et sanguinem perhorresce-
rent." Here, the more distinctly for contrast
with a different view, we have the idea entertained
by many (multi) of the sacrificial meaning at the
ground of these gladiatorial contests. But perhaps
the most remarkable instance in the August.
Hist. is that found in the Emperor Aurelian's
letter to the Roman Senate.[2] It is the very
heart of Pagan Imperial Rome speaking out in
its stern and superstitious soldier. " Miror vos
Patres sancti, tamdiu de aperienda Sybillinis dubi-
tasse libris, perinde quasi in Christianorum Ec-
clesia, non in templo deorum omnium tractraretis.

[1] 168 C.
[2] *Flav. Vopisci Syracus. Divus. Aurelianus*, 215 E.

Agite igitur et castimonia pontificum, ceremoniis-
que solennibus juvate principem necessitate pub-
lica laborantem. Inspiciantur libri; quæ facienda
fuerint celebrentur; quemlibet sumptum, cujuslibet
gentis captivos, qualibet animalia regia non abnuo
sed libens offero: Neque enim indecorum est
diis juvantibus vincere: sic apud majores nostros
multa finita sunt bella — sic coepta."

Claud. Salmasius, in a note upon this letter,
dwells on the recognized custom of consulting the
Sybilline Books, in extreme circumstances, with the
expectation of having to offer sacrifices by public
authority from which at other times they shrunk.

Porphyrius, who cannot be supposed to have
any disposition unfavorable to paganism, treats the
question of human sacrifices among the ancients
as a recognized fact to be reasoned about. In
particular he refers to the sacrifice mentioned by
Lactantius as something well known.[1]

Καὶ παρίημι Θρᾶκας καὶ Σκύθας, καὶ ὡς ᾿Αθηναῖοι τὴν ᾿Ερεχθέως
καὶ Πραξιθέας θυγατέρα ἀνεῖλον. ᾿Αλλ᾿ ἔτι γε νῦν τίς ἀγνοεῖ κατὰ τὴν
μεγάλην πόλιν τῇ τοῦ Λατιαρίου Διὸς ἑορτῇ σφαζόμενον ἄνθρωπον;[2]

This author seems to have had some weight
with Macaulay.

Eusebius, the ecclesiastical historian, has been

---

[1] *De Abstinentia*, lib. ii. 56.

[2] "And I do not mention the Thracians and Scythians, and how
the Athenians put to death the daughter of Erechtheus and Prax-
ithea. But even at the present day, who does not know that in the
great city on the festival of Jupiter Latiaris a man is slain?"

subjected to severe criticism, but he still retains authority on the most important matters of history. We may certainly receive his testimony when it agrees largely with other writers. In his treatment of human sacrifices, to which he gives several pages, he quotes several pagan writers, and amongst them Porphyry, distinguished for his opposition to Christianity. Thus, in Eusebius,[1] we have the very words of the pagan author already quoted from his own work " De Abstinent."

On page 157 D of the same book Eusebius refers to Clemens of Alexandria, and gives his statement before mentioned of the Athenian sacrifice, and also of that by the Roman Marius of his daughter to the deities Averrunci. Eusebius speaks of the abolition of human sacrifices by the Emperor Hadrian as matter of history, and distinctly claims for Christianity an influence on the paganism of the empire in this respect.

In Eusebius's " Eccles. Hist.,"[2] the tyrant Maxentius, among his other atrocities, is described as practicing magical arts and to that end "γυναῖκας ἐγκύμονας ἀνασχίζοντος τοτὲ δὲ, νεογνῶν σπλάγχνα βρέφων διερευνωμένου."[3]

The same account of Maxentius is given in Eusebius's " Vita Constant."[4]

---

[1] *Præpat. Evangel.*, lib. iv., 16, p. 156 C.
[2] Lib. viii., cap. xiv.
[3] " Ripping up women with child, and again examining the viscera of new-born babes."
[4] Lib. i., cap. 36.

There is another reference to the sacrifice of Jupiter Latiar. in "Orat. Euseb. de Laud. Constant.," where the same language as that used above is repeated. It is in connection with a long passage upon the atrocity of the practice. Evidently the writer dwelt upon what was well known and acknowledged to be true of Paganism. The ecclesiastical historian, Socrates, in lib. iii., cap. 2, gives an account of the revelation of immolations in Pagan sacrifices made by the discovery of a shrine in Alexandria.

Ἄδυτον ηὕρηται . . . . ἐν ᾧ τὰ μυστήρια τῶν Ἑλλήνων ἐκέκρυπτο ταῦτα δὲ ἦν κρανία ἀνθρώπων πολλὰ, νέων τε καὶ παλαιῶν, οὓς λόγος κατεῖχε πάλαι ἀναιρεῖσθαι, ὅτε ταῖς διὰ σπλάγχνων μαντείαις ἐχρῶντο οἱ Ἕλληνες, καὶ μαγικὰς ἐτέλουν θυσίας, καταμαγγανεύοντες τὰς ψυχάς.[1]

Exceptions will be taken, naturally, to the testimony against the Pagans borne by writers evidently so ready to believe the darkest stories told of heathen practices. But they narrate what was in itself not strange in that age of degenerate races and superstitions maddened by defeat, and what is merely a repetition of that affirmed by even non-Christian writers.

Whatever may be the personal credibility of

---

[1] "A shrine was found in which the mysteries of the Greeks had been concealed. Here there were many skulls of human beings, both young and old, and it is the report that they were slain anciently at the time when the Greeks practiced divination by inspection of the viscera, and used magic arts for invoking the shades."

the ecclesiastical historian, Theodoritus, the account he gives at least shows the belief held in his times by the Christians as to the practices of the revived Paganism. In " Theodorit. Episcopi Cyri. Eccles. Histor.,"[1] speaking of the Emperor Julian, Theodoritus says :

'Επεὶ δὲ ὁ θανατὸς ἀπηγγέλθη, καὶ εὐσεβὴς βασιλεία τὴν δυσεβῆ διεδέξατο, εἴσω γενόμενοι τοῦ σηκοῦ, εὖρον τὴν ἀξιάγαστον τοῦ βασιλέως ἀνδρείαν τε καὶ σοφιάν, καὶ πρὸς τούτοις εὐσέβειαν. Εἶδον γὰρ γύναιον ἐκ τῶν τριχῶν ἠωρωμένον, ἐκτεταμένας ἔχον τὰς χεῖρας ἧς ἀνακείρας ὁ ἀλιτήριος τὴν γαστέρα, τὴν νίκην δήπουθε κατὰ τῶν Περσῶν διὰ τοῦ ἥπατος ἔγνω.[2]

Again in 27 ch. : —

'Εν 'Αντιοχεία δέ, πολλὰς μὲν κιβωτοὺς ἐν τοῖς βασιλείοις κεφαλῶν ἀνθρώπων πεπληρωμένας εὑρῆσθαί φασι, πολλὰ δὲ φρέατα σωμάτων ἀνάπλεα νεκρῶν, τοιαῦτα γὰρ δυσωνύμων Θεῶν τὰ μαθήματα.[3]

Cyril, in his lib. iv., " Contr. Julian," dwells very fully upon the prevalence of human sacrifices in Paganism, and says of the gladiatorial contests :[4]—

---

[1] Lib. iii. 26.

[2] " But after his death was announced, and a pious reign had succeeded the impious one, they entered the sanctuary and discovered the proofs of the wonderful courage and wisdom of the prince, nay, even of his piety. For they saw a woman hanging by the hair, and with hands extended. After cutting open her belly, the wretch had divined his victory over the Persians by inspection of her liver."

[3] " In Antioch, moreover, they say that many chests were found in the palace, filled with human heads, and many wells full of dead bodies. For such were the teachings of the abominable gods."

[4] Page 128 D.

Ἐν ἀκμαῖς δὲ οὔσης ἔτι τῆς Ἑλληνικῆς δεισιδαιμονίας, ἅμιλλαι μονομαχίας ἐπετελοῦντο παρὰ Ῥωμαίοις κατὰ καιρούς· κέκρυπτο δὲ τις ὑπὸ γῆν Κρόνος λίθοις τετρημένοις ὑποκεχηνὼς, ἵνα τῷ τοῦ πεσόντος καταμιαίνοιτο λύθρῳ.[1]

In the same book[2] Cyril meets an evasion which does not affect the substance of his charge.

Ἀλλ' ὦ βέλτιστοι, φαίη ἄν, εἰ μὴ θεοῖς μᾶλλον, καθάπερ αὐτοὶ διατείνεσθε, δαίμοσι δὲ πονηροῖς καὶ ἀποτροπαίοις τὰς δι' αἱμάτων θυσίας προσεκόμιζον οἱ παλαιοὶ, οὐκ ἀνθρώπων μόνον ἀλλὰ καὶ ζώων ἀλόγων τίσιν ἄρα τοὺς ἀνὰ πᾶσαν χώράν τε καὶ πόλιν ἀνεδείμασθε ναοὺς, καὶ τοὺς ἐν αὐτοῖς ἱδρύσασθε βωμούς ; καίτοι πῶς οὐχ ἅπασιν ἐναργὲς, ὡς ἐν ἱερῷ παντὶ, καὶ μέχρι τῶν καθ' ἡμᾶς καιρῶν τὰς θυσίας ἐτέλουν, καὶ οὐκ ἦν ἐν αὐτοῖς οὐ μικρὸς, οὐ μέγας, οὐκ ἰδιώτης, οὐ σοφὸς, οὐ τῶν ἐν ὑπεροχαῖς ἀξιωμάτων, οὐ τῶν ἐν ὑφέσει καὶ οὐδὲν ἐχόντων ἀξιάκουστον, ὃς οὐ πάντη τε καὶ πάντως ταῖς οὕτως αἰσχραῖς καὶ φιλαιμάτοις θυσίαις ἐχρήσατο.[3]

Again, in lib. vi.[4] he reproaches Julian with

[1] And while the superstition of the Greeks was in full vigor, gladiatorial combats were practiced among the Romans on stated occasions. A certain representation of Saturn had been concealed under the earth, yawning beneath perforated stones, in order that (through them) he might be defiled with the blood of the slain man."

[2] Lib. iv., p. 130 B.

[3] " But, my good sirs—some one may say, if the ancients, as you contend, did not offer bloody sacrifices, not only of men, but also of brute beasts, to the gods, but rather to the evil and abominable divinities, for whom then have you built temples in every land and city, and set up the altars within them ? In truth, is it not clear to all, that in every temple, even up to our time, they have performed sacrifices, and that there was not in them one, small or great, wise or simple, high in honor, or of low estate, and of no reputation, who did not, in every possible way, make use of these sacrifices so shameful and bloody ! "

[4] Page 197.

the pleasure his gods took in such a sacrifice as the Roman Marius was believed to have offered.

Ἐπαρίθμει δὲ αὐτὸ τοῖς ἐκ Θεῶν ἀγαθοῖς καὶ τὸ δεδόσθαι Ῥωμαίοις τὸν Μάριον, βασιλεύσαντα μὲν κατὰ καιροὺς δεισιδαιμονέστατον δὲ καὶ ἀπηνῆ γεγονότα, καὶ μὴν καὶ ἀγρίου φρονήματος καθιγμένον εἰς τοῦτο, ὥστε τὸ εὖ τεθραμμένον αὐτῷ κόριον, καὶ τὸ ὅτι μάλιστα τῶν φιλτάτον, ἐπιχάρι τε καὶ γλυκὺ, τοῖς τῶν δαιμονίων ἐγκατάσφάξαι βωμοῖς.[1]

Cyril's spirit, as displayed in controversy even with the Pagans, cannot be admired ; but we must bear in mind the atrocities with which he had to deal.   Yet, however severely we judge him for his hard and bigot nature, we must believe his testimony when it agrees with other Christian writers upon what was matter of recognition to them all.

Gregory Nazianzenus, in his orations against Julian, gives a fearful picture of the Pagan emperor.   Of course, his invective is an exaggeration, and we cannot wonder that to the eyes of Christians the restorer of Paganism must have appeared in the worst possible light, particularly after years of ingenious devices to crush out Christianity in his empire and to reëstablish Paganism.   For they knew its abominations.   Whether Julian himself

---

[1] "Count this truly among the favors of the gods that Marius has been given to the Romans, once indeed their master, but excelling in superstition and cruelty.   Indeed he brought himself to such a harshness of temper, that he slew at the altars of the gods a girl well born and bred, and who was one of those most dear to himself and both gracious and pleasing."

was guilty of practicing the bloody rites alleged against him, there is little doubt that they existed at his time. Gregory's reference to them is found in " Orat. Tertia Advers. Jul."[1]: —

Σιωπήσομαι τὸν Ὀρόντην, καὶ τοὺς νυκτερινοὺς νεκροὺς, οὓς τῷ βασιλεῖ συνέκρυπτεν οὗτος στεινόμενος νεκύεσσι καὶ κτείων ἀδήλως · ἐνταῦθα γὰρ τὰ τοῦ ἔπους οἰκειότερον · παραδραμοῦμαι καὶ τῶν βασιλείων καὶ τὰ κοῖλα καὶ ἀπωτάτω, ὅσα τε ἐν λάκκοις, καὶ φρέασι, καὶ διώρυξι, κακῶν γέμοντα θεσαύρων τε καὶ μυστηρίων, οὐ μόνον τῶν ἀνατεμνομένων παίδων τε καὶ παρθένων ἐπὶ ψυχαγωγίᾳ καὶ μαντείᾳ, καὶ θυσίαις οὐ νενομισμέναις ἀλλὰ καὶ τῶν ὑπὲρ εὐσεβείας κινδυνευόντων.[2]

Athanasius also, in his " Orat. Adver. Gentes," fol. 21, refers to the Latiarian sacrifice: " Καὶ, οἱ πάλαι δὲ Ῥωμαῖοι τὸν καλούμενον Λατιάριον Δία ἀνθρωπυσίαις ἐθρήσκευον."[3]

The passages in Orosius already referred to are lib. iv., cap. 13: " Gallum virum et Gallam fæminam cum muliere simul Græca in foro boario vivos defoderunt; " the instance, with a slight difference, recorded by Livy and others; also lib. v.,

[1] Page 91 C.

[2] " I will not mention the Orontes, and the dead slain by night which it concealed for the emperor, filled as it was with corpses and bringing death secretly, for here the words of the epic strain would be more fitting. I will also pass by the cavernous and far-remote dungeons of the palace, the cellars, wells, and trenches filled with evil treasures and mysteries, not only with boys and girls who had been cut open for an invocation to the shades, and for divination, and for sacrifices not legitimate, — but even with those whose lives were sought because of their piety."

[3] " And the ancient Romans worshipped the so called Jupiter Latiaris with human sacrifices."

cap. 24, where Orosius treats briefly of the war of the gladiators and fugitives under Spartacus and Crixus. " In exsequis captivæ matronæ, quæ se dolore violati pudoris necaverat, munus gladiatorum ex quadringentis captivis, scilicet qui spectandi fuerant spectaturi, utpote lanistæ, gladiatorum potius quam militum principes, ediderunt."

Ammianus Marcellus, who lived in the time of Julian, in his history refers to bloody rites still practiced, as connected with soothsaying. Thus he speaks [1] of " Pollentianum tribunum malitia quemdam exsuperantem, iisdem diebus convictum confessumque quod exsecto vivæ mulieris ventre, atque in tempestivo partu extracto, infernis manibus excitis de permutatione imperii consulere ausus est."

The following extract from Prudentius,[2] makes prominent the sacrificial character of the gladiatorial combats and the Latiarian offering, conclusively showing the author's conviction that these were human sacrifices and as such were urged against the celebrated plea for the Paganism of Rome.

> " Respice terrifici scelerata sacraria Ditis,
> Cui cadit infausta fusus gladiator arena,   ·
> Heu male lustratæ Phlegethontia victima Romæ,
> Namquid vesani sibi vult ars impia ludi?
> Quid mortes juvenum? quid sanguine pasta voluptas?
> Quid pulvis caveæ semper funebris, et illa

---

[1] Lib. xxix. 11.
[2] *Contra Symmachi Oratio,* lines 379–399.

Amphitheatralis spectacula tristia Pompæ?
Nempe Charon jugulis miserorum se duce dignas,
Accipit inferios, placatus crimine sacro,
Hæ sunt deliciæ Jovis infernalis : in istis
Arbiter obscuri placidus requiescit Averni.
Nonne pudet regem populum sceptris potentem
Talia pro patriæ censere litanda salute?
Religionis opem subternis poscere ab antris?
Evocat, heu, pœnis tenebrosa ex sede ministrum
Interitiis, speciosa hominum cui funera solvat,
Incassum arguere jam Taurica sacra solemus :
Funditur humanus Latiari in munere sanguis,
Consessusque ille spectantium solvit ad aram
Plutonis fera vota sui, quid sanctius ara,
Quæ bibit egestum per mystica tela cruorem?"

Macrobius, who wrote as late as Honorius, in his "Saturnal."[1] refers to human sacrifices offered to Mania, as "restituti scilicet a Tarquinio superbo Laribus et Maniæ, ex responso Apollinis: quo præceptum est ut pro capitibus, capitibus supplicaretur, idque aliquandiu observatum ut pro familiarium sospitate pueri mactarentur Maniæ deæ matri Larum quod sacrificii genus Junius Brutus consul Tarquinio pulso aliter constituit celebrandum, nam capitibus alii et papaveris supplicari jussit, ut responso Apollinis satisfieret."

In lib. iii., ch. 7, he speaks of what is referred to by Livy and others as "ver sacrum." "Hoc loco non alienum videtur de conditione eorum hominum referre, quos leges sacros esse certis diis jubenti quia non ignoro quibusdam mirum videri quod cum cætera sacra violari nefas sit hominem

---

[1] Liber i., ch. 7.

sacrum jus fuerit occidi, cujus rei causa hæc est veteres nullum animal sacrum in finibus suis esse patiebatur, sed abigebant ad fines deorum quibus sacrum esset : animas vero , sacratorum hominum, quos Græci ζωάνας vocant, dis debitas æstimabant. Quemadmodum igitur quod ad deos ipsos mitti non poterat a se tamen dimittere non dubitabant; sic animas quas sacras in cœlum mitti posse arbitrati sunt viduatas corpore quam primum illo ire voluerunt." Upon this passage Gronovius remarks in a note : " ' Hominem sacrum jus fuerit occidi ' Lex Tribunicia ; 'SI QUIS. IMP. QUI PLEBISSCITO. SACER. SIT. OCCIDERIT. PARRICIDA. NE. SIT.' Vid Estium in Sacer mons et in ver sacrum. Budæus in Commentario Linguæ Græcæ ' Anathemata dicti sacri homines, quorum capita diis inferis dicata et devota, vide an huc spectet illud Pauli ad Rom. cap. 9 : 3, optantes pro fratribus fieri anathema.' " As stated above, other objects were later substituted for human beings in a sacrifice liable to be on a frightful scale, but the continued remembrance of the original offering shows the place held by the idea in the Pagan mind.

The Theodosian Code has been thought by some to contain the prohibition of human sacrifices. One passage referred to is that in lib. xvi., tit. 10, " Theod. Valent. lex adv. Sacr." x.: " Nemo se hostiis polluat, nemo insontem victimam cædat "— but a word of similar meaning to " in-

sontem " (innoxiorum) is applied to animals by
Arnobius.[1]

In a note upon 11 Imp. Constantius A., ad
Madel. aq. vic. P. T. P., where the expression
"Sacrificiorum aboleatur insania" had occurred,
we read " Quare hoc insaniæ verbo non animales
tantum hostiæ, vel humana sacrificia traducuntur,
sed quæcumque tandem sacrificia." In another
note on the same law another commentator writes,
after quoting Cyrillus and other writers as affirming the existence of human sacrifices down to the
time of Constantine : " Nec igitur Hadriani lex
humanas hostias prohibens, auctore Lact. d. c. 21,
rebus et factis recepta fuerat, Constantinus autem
sacrificia penitus sustulit, ut nominatum hac leg.
continetur, quod etiam Constantius confirmat."

Zonaras writes much later, but it may be worth
while to quote from his history. In tome ii., he
reäffirms the statement in the Augustæ Historiæ
Scriptor concerning Heliogabalus : Καὶ οὐ μόνον
βαρβαρικὰς ὠδὰς ἅμα τῇ μητρὶ καὶ τῇ τηθῃ τῷ ξένῳ
θεῷ αὐτοῦ ἥδε καὶ ἀπορρήτους προσῆγε θυσίας, παῖδας
σφαγιάζων. [2]

In lib. xiii. 7, we find the following : Ὁ δὲ Μαγνέν-
τιος καὶ γοητείαις ἐχρήσατο. Γυνὴ γάρ τις μάγος,
παρθένον αὐτῷ σφαγιάσαι ὑπέθετο καὶ οἴνῳ τὸ ταύτης

---

[1] Lib. vii.

[2] "And he not only sung barbaric songs with his mother and
grandmother to his strange god, and introduced forbidden sacrifices, slaying boys."

αἷμα προσμίξαι καὶ δοῦναι τοῖς στρατιώταις αὐτὸ ἀπογεύσασθαι.[1]

From these and kindred passages in the literature of antiquity so many have drawn the conclusion that human sacrifices existed among the Romans down to a late period. Their best men indeed abhorred it, and at different times the practice was publicly forbidden. But it was too deeply rooted in the Pagan mind to cease till Christian civilization completely displaced the system of which it formed a part. We are the more inclined to believe this because there can be no question of its prevalence in other nations. The ground of this lies deep in human nature and hath an awful significance for any one who studies profoundly our race and its moral relations. Besides such a practice was in singular harmony with the Roman character. We must not let our admiration for Rome and her achievements blind us to the monstrous wickedness of the national heart. Her Ciceros and Senecas and Antonines cannot redeem the "wolves of Italy" from moral reprobation. If any regard Paul's description of heathenesse in the Empire as exaggerated, let him for a while forget strength and order to study Roman manners in her writers. The vileness they describe and imply is something unintelligi-

---

[1] " Magnentius also practiced witchcraft, for a certain sorceress counseled him to slay a maiden, to mingle her blood with wine, and to give this to the soldiers to taste."

ble ; Paul's terrible sentences are mildness to some
of these passages. But the hardness of the Roman
heart is a study by itself. Perhaps in our system
of strange compensation this was the certain evil
condition of their unexampled success. Nevertheless Roman hardness has never been equaled.
Recall their history. They came into existence
fighting. They lived to fight. Trace their course
into empire. Remark their proscriptions. Im-
agine that Roman city when its centralization was
greatest. Forget its splendid palaces and plun-
dered statues. Turn from its glittering triumphs
with their trophies of victory and trains of captives.
Behold all this gorgeous display ending with cold-
blooded murder. Look at its vast populace fed
on alms and amused with human slaughter, beg-
gars and butchers at once. If in æsthetic Greece
refinement and a certain sensibility could not pre-
vent human sacrifices from lingering long in its
Paganism, it is only reasonable to expect that such
a nature as the Roman, gorged with blood, and
delighting in homicide, would retain till the end the
most cruel rite of their religion. Hence we are more
ready to believe the rhetorician Lactantius than
the rhetorician Macaulay, and listen more com-
placently to the pleasant jingle of the latter's lays
than to his judgment of the morals of ancient
Rome. If we do not suffer the high civilization
and fruitful Christianity of parts of English society
to hide from us the almost heathen grossness and

brutality of other portions, much less may we doubt the alleged atrocities of society like that of Rome. Strange that any Christian student with the classics before him can question the chief application of John's revelation to ancient Rome as it appeared to the eyes of Christian truth in his day. Strange, too, it seems in the history of our faith that men presumed to make so foul a place as Rome the capital of Christendom, and one cannot help thinking that there is a dreadful irony in her name of the Eternal City. It may be a wild imagination, and yet we are tempted sometimes to believe that the spirit of that heathen past never left its abode, but remained a hidden Nemesis to punish men for building on impossible foundations.

NOTE.

———◆———

WHEN pp. 36–38 of this work, containing the extracts from Merivale's history, were going through the press, the author was not aware of what that historian had said elsewhere upon this subject. But in a note to his Boyle Lecture, Merivale expresses himself more positively than in his history : —

"So strong is the protest of Roman civilization against it, that on a superficial view of the facts it has been often asserted, that human sacrifice was actually abolished for centuries under the sway of the Roman emperors. Such was, however, far from the case. Even in the state ritual of Rome some traces of the practice still continued to linger. Even on public occasions and national objects, human sacrifices were from time to time offered. Still worse, the practice creeps back again for private and personal objects, and is associated with magical ceremonies. When the state is merged in the ruler it is difficult to distinguish the personal from the public interest, but it was probably more for their own sake than for the sake of the commonwealth, that irregular sacrifices of this kind were perpetrated by Julius Cæsar, by Augustus, by Tiberius, and Nero ; and after them still more frequently, and without disguise, by most of the succeeding emperors. Trajan himself sacrificed a beautiful woman after the earthquake as a propitiation, we may suppose, for the safety of that city. The self-devotion of Antinous for Hadrian is an instance of quasi sacrifice. . . . . The calamities of the state seemed to demand greater and more striking efforts to appease the manifest wrath of Heaven. Along with the increase of other wild and gloomy superstitions human sacrifices became more and more common. . . . .

"The execution of the Christians was thus popularly regarded as a means of propitiation. This idea was sanctioned and fostered, apparently, by the most usual manner of these executions; for the shows of the amphitheatre had sprung out of the primitive custom of sacrificing human victims at the altar of a god, or the tomb of a deceased hero. Even to the time of Constantine, it is said, a vestige of this idea was preserved in the annual immolation of a gladiator on the Alban Mount to Jupiter Latiaris."